"Through the curation of poignant testimonies and reflections from local Ferguson clergy and activists, Dr. Gunning Francis has created a pathway for the construction of practical theologies that will inform and shape the prophetic leadership of preachers, pastors, and faith-based organizers in the ongoing struggle for freedom, justice, and peace in our communities."

—Michael Ray Mathews, Director of Clergy Organizing, PICO National Network

"Words—hard words, blunt words, truthful words, empowering words—Words of God. Leah Gunning Francis enlivens sacred stories of religious leaders—old and young—as they confront 'systemic evil.' Using the best of qualitative research and practical theology, Dr. Gunning Francis records the words faithful people use to connect the 'resources' of faith traditions, personal skills, and passionate hearts into actions. The clues we encounter call us to search, to live, and to enflesh the 'words of God.'"

—Jack Seymour, Garrett-Evangelical Theological Seminary

"While the Church often overplays its role in the Civil Rights Movement, its contributions to that freedom struggle have nevertheless been tangible and transformative. How will the faith community be remembered for its response to the Black Lives Matter movement that is aggressive and sometimes profane, non-hierarchical, and wary of organized religion? Rooted in St. Louis, Leah Gunning Francis effectively weaves together profiles of local Christian and Jewish leaders who, inspired by the Ferguson moment, are working to creatively disrupt white supremacy in their religious institutions and the wider society."

—Ethan Vesely-Flad, Director of National Organizing, Fellowship of Reconciliation

"The movement that sprung from the ground where Michael Brown's body lay is one of diverse voices brought together by a common call. There was no owner's manual, no rules on the back of the game box, just people compelled by their faith sense of justice to stay silent no longer. Dr. Gunning Francis powerfully brings those voices together and lets them tell the story of the first days of this new civil rights movement."

—Michael Kinman, Dean of Christ Church Cathedral, St. Louis

"Leah Gunning Francis, as a mother of two young African American sons, a clergy spouse, and a seminary professor, resolves to make audible the voices of twenty-four clergy and thirteen young leaders at ground zero in Ferguson, Missouri, in the aftermath of the shooting death of Michael Brown. With vivid and breathtaking prose, she shares their stories of lived faith on the frontlines of injustice that forms a seamless vestment of justice and hope. Specifically, Francis focuses on clergy leadership who through interaction with young movement leaders where compelled to embody their faith commitments in the midst of teargas and rubber bullets wielded by police and the National Guard. Professor Gunning Francis helps clergypersons answer the question: How must I live my faith when injustice brings tragedy to the community? This book is required reading for clergypersons serving in congregations and social agencies regardless of their social location as well as required reading for seminary students preparing for leadership in faith-based communities. Lastly, this book is essential reading for all those seeking to weave together a spiritual, political, and social life that is sacred and consistent with the Gospel of Jesus Christ."

—Evelyn Parker, Perkins School of Theology

"This is a very important book. Leah Gunning Francis has penned a theological memoir of a movement. It is an invitation to see the spirituality at the heart of this movement. And it is an invitation to get into the streets...since we don't just change the world with our heads, but with our hands and feet and sweat and tears. One of the most important things this book does is celebrate a new generation of activists and faith-rooted organizers, without forgetting the freedom-fighters of old. This is not your granny's revolution. A fresh, new, holy uprising is happening if we will only have eyes to see and ears to hear—and the courage to join them in the streets."

—Shane Claiborne, Author, Speaker, Activist

"Their work was a work of justice. This volume is a work of justice too, as it allows us to hear the voices of both the young activists and the clergy who were on the streets of Ferguson during those stressful weeks and months. The ecclesiology that emerges from these testimonies is compelling. This is a must-read for all leaders of faith communities. In addition, this is a model for the power of qualitative research to change the narrative. Because Leah Gunning Francis has allowed the voices of these leaders to speak through her pages, we have a completely different picture of what was happening in Ferguson, Missouri, in 2014. Her work allows us to hear and see the vocation of the church, of the clergy, and of all children on God."

—Margaret Ann Crain, Garrett-Evangelical Theological Seminary

"This book is a powerful collection of stories of clergy and young activists who were visible and vocal in the struggle for racial justice in Ferguson. They embodied the best of the human spirit that resonated with many around the globe, and challenged this nation to live up to its ideal of liberty and justice for all."

—Emanuel Cleaver, U.S. Representative (Missouri)

"Leah Gunning Francis—seminary professor, activist, mother, and church leader—offers an on-the-ground account of the Ferguson, Missouri, protests rocking the nation in the aftermath of the killing of Michael Brown. Through interviews with church leaders and young people participating in the outcry for justice, Gunning-Francis offers a story of Ferguson largely untold by news media accounts. It is a story beginning in her own experience as the mother of two sons. She uses her passion from her personal stake in the police killings of African American young men as the jumping-off point for faith-based activism in the events of Ferguson, and for interviews with St. Louis area church leaders. The story she tells is one of church leaders in solidarity with young people as together they demanded change and were willing to put themselves at risk to make their voices heard. Gunning Francis paints a compelling picture of theology in action as people of faith joined together not only to express their outrage but ultimately in the hopes of confronting and transforming racism in America."

—Joyce Mercer, Virginia Theological Seminary

FERGUSON & FAITH

Sparking Leadership & Awakening Community

LEAH GUNNING FRANCIS

CHALICE
PRESS

ST. LOUIS, MISSOURI

Cover art and design: Bidemi (Bd) Oladele

www.ChalicePress.com

Paperback: 9780827211056

EPUB: 9780827211063   EPDF: 9780827211070

Library of Congress Cataloging-in-Publication Data

Francis, Leah Gunning.
Ferguson and faith : sparking leadership and awakening community / by Leah Gunning Francis. — First Edition.
    pages cm
Includes bibliographical references and index.
ISBN 978-0-8272-1105-6 (pbk. : alk. paper)
1. Protest movements—Missouri—Ferguson. 2. Social movements— Religious aspects. 3. Community development—Missouri—Ferguson. I. Title.
HN59.2.F73 2015
303.48'40977865—dc23
                    2015022562

Contents

Editor's Foreword

Cultivating Faithful, Wise and Courageous Leaders for the Church and Academy

Welcome to a conversation at the intersection of young adults, faith, and leadership. The Forum for Theological Exploration (FTE) is a leadership incubator that inspires diverse young people to make a difference in the world through Christian communities. This series, published in partnership with Chalice Press, is for individuals reimagining Christian leadership and creating innovative approaches to ministry and scholarship from diverse contexts.

These books are written by and for a growing network of:

- FTE partners seeking to cultivate Christian leaders, pastors, and theological educators needed to renew and respond to a changing church.

- Young leaders exploring traditional and alternative paths to ministry and teaching that serve the common good and justice—both inside and beyond "the walls" of the church and theological academy.

- Christian leaders developing new ways to awaken the search for meaning and purpose in young adults who are inspired to shape the future of the church, academy, and world.

- Members and leaders of faith communities creating new solutions to address the needs of their congregations, institutions, and the broader community.

This series offers an opportunity to discover what FTE is learning, widen the circle of conversation, and share ideas FTE believes are necessary for faith communities to shape a more hopeful future.

Thank you for joining us!

Dori Baker, Series Editor
Stephen Lewis, FTE President

Foreword

by Jim Wallis

Ferguson and Faith is a frontline account of the experiences of young activist leaders and local clergy—the two groups who have played the biggest role in transforming the aftermath of Michael Brown's tragic death from a *moment* to a *movement*. To create this book, Leah Gunning Francis interviewed dozens of clergy and young leaders, from diverse religious and racial backgrounds, who found themselves united in a desire to confront and transform a criminal justice system—and broader society—that systematically values black and brown lives less than it values white lives. The brave young women and men in Ferguson took their convictions to the streets and laid their safety—and indeed their very lives—on the line day after day in the face of a police response more suitable for a theater of war than the streets of an American city. They refused to let tear gas or rubber bullets silence their voices. And when the clergy interviewed in this book joined those young leaders, they also put themselves in situations of risk. Tear gas and rubber bullets shape theology, as you will read in this important volume. This is what happens when we take faith to the streets.

At Sojourners' annual leadership Summit in 2015, many of these young leaders and clergy were honored. The theme of the Summit was leadership and hope—and these young people and clergy demonstrated both. Hope means getting up, day after day and night after night, and getting back at the struggle for freedom and justice. That's what these activists and clergy did in the face of both exhaustion and danger. And that's what leadership means. Each honoree received a small wooden holding cross, a perfect thing to hold in our hands when we are leading with hope in ways that drive us to risk taking.

I believe that if the young Ferguson leaders hadn't gotten up day after day and gone to the streets night after night, and some courageous clergy hadn't joined them there and spoken out in their community, there might never have been a historic national commission on policing or a damning Department of Justice report on the Ferguson Police Department—and we would not be at the beginning of a new national conversation on reforming the criminal justice system. But it is only the beginning, and the test of the nation's soul will be action aimed at the systemic racial injustice embedded in that system. Without the courage and perseverance of the young Ferguson activists and clergy, we simply would not be in the place of new possibilities that we now find ourselves. While the road ahead of us to achieve racial freedom, equity, and healing is still long and difficult, I believe that future generations may well look back on the Ferguson movement as a watershed in our painful racial history. The young leaders and clergy who led the way may be seen as key figures who helped bend the arc of history toward justice, much as the civil rights movement did in the 1960s.

Leah Gunning Francis's conversations with both the clergy and the young activists show how important it is for communities of faith to reach out to a new generation of young leaders and help elevate and nurture their gifts. What many of the clergy interviewed in this book realized in the course of the Ferguson protests was that rather than sitting back in their sanctuaries and waiting for the young people to seek out the church for guidance or leadership, it was *the church* that needed to go out and meet the young people where they were, joining them shoulder to shoulder, on the streets, in the struggle for justice.

Equally important, the clergy did not go out there expecting automatically to lead or be listened to simply by virtue of being clergy. They understood that these young protestors were *already* leaders who were accomplishing extraordinary things, and that they needed *allies* in the clergy more than they needed the clergy to act as their leaders. At the same time, by meeting these young leaders where they were and being their allies in the truest sense of the word, these clergy were able to use their gifts, experience, and networks to complement and elevate the gifts and experience of the young activists.

From churches that were distrusted for their distance and isolation from the lives and experience of marginalized young people came clergy willing to be transformed by their engagement in the streets, some of whom became role models and pastors for new generation activists whose trust they had gained. Ferguson is one of the best examples of the authenticity and power that come from walking our talk.

While many books will be written on the complex issues surrounding the killing of Michael Brown, the racism of the Ferguson Police Department, the Black Lives Matter movement, this is not one of those books. Rather, this book is a collection of *stories* of people on the front lines of a struggle against profound societal injustices at a historically significant moment in time. What this book offers is nothing more or less than the direct experiences and perspectives of those who were there. I believe that stories are critically important to the ongoing struggle for racial justice, and I have seen many times that it is the experience of hearing and *believing* the stories of others that causes people's own perspectives to be transformed.

This book shows that clergy can make a real difference in today's social movements if we are willing to leave our comfort zones, take our faith to the streets, and are humble enough to open ourselves to learning from a new generation that is now leading the way in many of the most important struggles to overcome racial injustice. I invite you to learn from these extraordinary stories, and be inspired to join in these struggles.

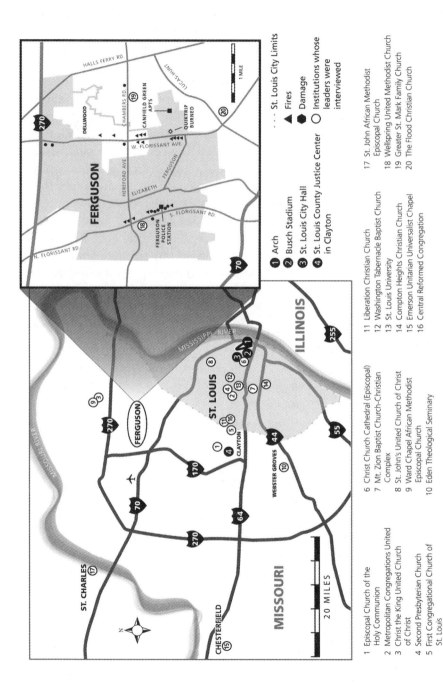

MISSOURI

20 MILES

N

ST. CHARLES 17

CHESTERFIELD 15

FERGUSON

ST. LOUIS

CLAYTON

WEBSTER GROVES 10

MISSISSIPPI RIVER

MISSOURI RIVER

ILLINOIS

FERGUSON

HALLS FERRY RD

DELLWOOD

CHAMBERS RD.

CANFIELD GREEN APTS

QUIKTRIP BURNED

W. FLORISSANT AVE.

HEREFORD AVE.

ELIZABETH

S. FLORISSANT RD.

FERGUSON POLICE STATION

N. FLORISSANT RD

LUCAS-HUNT

1 MILE

- - - St. Louis City Limits
▲ Fires
⬡ Damage
○ Institutions whose leaders were interviewed

1 Arch
2 Busch Stadium
3 St. Louis City Hall
4 St. Louis County Justice Center in Clayton

1 Episcopal Church of the Holy Communion
2 Metropolitan Congregations United
3 Christ the King United Church of Christ
4 Second Presbyterian Church
5 First Congregational Church of St. Louis

6 Christ Church Cathedral (Episcopal)
7 Mt. Zion Baptist Church-Christian Complex
8 St. John's United Church of Christ
9 Ward Chapel African Methodist Episcopal Church
10 Eden Theological Seminary

11 Liberation Christian Church
12 Washington Tabernacle Baptist Church
13 St. Louis University
14 Compton Heights Christian Church
15 Emerson Unitarian Universalist Chapel
16 Central Reformed Congregation

17 St. John African Methodist Episcopal Church
18 Wellspring United Methodist Church
19 Greater St. Mark Family Church
20 The Flood Christian Church

Introduction

*"We have a powerful potential in our youth, and we must have
the courage to change old ideas and practices so that we may
direct their power toward good ends."*

Mary McLeod Bethune (1875–1955) Educator, Civil Rights
Activists, Humanitarian

August 9, 2014, started as an ordinary Saturday morning. Hot,
sunny, and just right for enjoying the final days of summer vacation.
After breakfast, I took our two sons to a friend's birthday party at a local
kids' play zone. While the children played, I chatted with other parents
about our summer adventures and how we were anxiously preparing for
the impending first day of school. We mused over lunchbox ideas and
afterschool activities, and wondered aloud how some of our children
would fare in their new schools. "Leaving kindergarten is a big step,"
one parent said, "I hope he finds his footing pretty quickly." "Me too,"
I said, as I thought about our youngest son leaving the cozy cocoon of
his preschool and venturing into the new terrain of elementary school.

Meanwhile, the children played, ate pizza and cake, and played
some more until they reluctantly had say their goodbyes. We hugged
and high-fived our friends as we made our way into our van. It was
still daylight and my sons were still pretty hyped from the party, so I
knew I needed to find a way to keep the party spirit going. We drove to
a nearby store and purchased a few school supplies and knick-knacks,
went home, ate dinner, and they played baseball in our backyard until
the August moon was ready to appear.

After the boys were bathed and in bed, I walked into the family
room and caught a glimpse of a chaotic scene on the evening news. As
I inched closer to the television, I suddenly heard: "You took my son
away from me! Do you know how hard it was for me to get him to stay

in school and graduate? You know how many black men graduate? Not many. Because you bring them down to this type of level, where they feel like they don't got nothing to live for anyway… But I refused to let my son be like that."[1] I stood, shell-shocked, in front of the television as I watched who I now know was Leslie McSpadden uttering those painful words to KMOV St. Louis reporter Brittany Noble on the fateful day her son, Michael Brown, Jr., was shot and killed by Ferguson, Missouri, police officer Darren Wilson. The police shooting of Michael Brown was the lead story on the local news and, at that time, the details were still murky and the circumstances were largely unknown. I had no idea what lay ahead.

The news images captured some of the chaos and anguish that gripped the Canfield Green apartment community where Brown was killed. In my mind, I kept trying to make sense of what was unfolding before my eyes. I had far more questions than answers. Witnesses were being interviewed and said that Brown had his hands up in surrender when he was killed, and that his body was left in the middle of this residential street for more than four hours. Children could be seen standing near the yellow crime scene tape that cordoned off the area. What began as a typical Saturday for me quickly morphed into something unusual, and once I saw an image of Brown's body lying face down on the pavement with his blood streaming down the middle of the street, I was convinced that life in St. Louis would never be quite the same.

I live in the city of St. Louis with my husband and our two sons. The city of Ferguson is a nearby northern suburb of St. Louis. Our house, which is on the south side of St. Louis, is only 11 miles from the Canfield Green apartment community where Michael Brown was killed. During my first visit to the apartment complex, two observations stopped me in my tracks. First, I was stunned by the narrowness of the street on which Brown was killed. I had been closely following the news coverage of the unfolding events for two days, and on television the street looked much wider than it actually is. Canfield Drive looked like a familiar street because it is not much wider than my own street— the same kind of street that my own sons ride their bikes along. The second startling observation was that this is an apartment *community*. It is privately owned, complete with manicured lawns and trimmed

---

[1] http://www.kmov.com/special-coverage-001/video/Michael-Browns-mother-speaks-right-after-shooting-272803691.html

bushes. There is ample green space for children to play and frolic around, and the location where Brown was killed is in the middle of this community. Apartment units are clustered on both sides of the street. As I stood beside the street memorial where Brown's body once lay, the gravity of what actually happened permeated my mind, body, and spirit: Michael Brown, an unarmed 18-year-old black man, was killed by a police officer in the middle of the day, in the middle of the street, in the middle of this residential community and laid there for over four hours for all to see. In that moment, I was awakened to a reality that was more than I could bear.

As the days, weeks, and months passed, I concluded that it was actually more than I could bear—I could not bear to sit quietly by and pretend that this was just another "unfortunate incident" or "ill-fated tragedy." I could not bear to go on with my days as though I had not seen, heard, and felt the cries of Brown's family and friends. I could not bear to allow my righteous indignation to remain locked inside my heart and mind, and not give voice to it through tangible acts of resistance. So I marched, prayed, organized, held vigil, lectured, protested, and passed out supplies—all in an attempt to bear witness to this tragedy and work toward social change. And I was not alone.

As a seminary professor and pastor's wife, I have deep ties to the progressive Christian community in the St. Louis area. I have worked with or visited dozens of congregations, and made connections with twice as many clergy throughout the region from almost every mainline denomination. As a woman of faith, I did not separate my actions in pursuit of justice for Michael Brown from my faith. Instead, I understood them as an expression of my faith. My faith, or my belief and trust in God, motivated me to join the efforts to seek justice and provide care. My faith was integral to my works, and, together, enabled me to embody my idea of faithfulness in this time of communal distress. Throughout the days, weeks, and months since Michael Brown was killed, there were many other people of faith who were taking similar and greater actions. Specifically, I am talking about clergypeople.

There were clergypeople involved in this movement since "day one." Of course there were scores of people who were neither clergy nor expressed a faith impetus for their participation in this movement, but I was compelled to try to keep my finger on the pulse of what local clergy were up to and join them. I took some of my direction from and worked with several of them; I learned from them and prayed for them as many were putting their bodies on the line in extremely risky ways. These were women and men whose primary places of service were in local congregations, jails, hospitals, seminaries, and nonprofit agencies, yet they made it their business to extend their services of care, hospitality, and vigilance into the streets of Ferguson and its environs.

Images of tanks and tear gas have flashed across television and computer screens around the world, but it is not likely that the breadth and diversity of stories of clergy that laid their all on the altar of justice ever made it across the airwaves in a comprehensive way. This book shines a spotlight on some of their sacred stories of courage and hope that might awaken in us seeds of possibilities that, if nurtured, could bend our imagination and actions toward a future filled with hope. This book, however, does not pretend to represent all of the clergy that have participated in or contributed to the movement for justice for Michael Brown, as there are untold numbers of clergy that have supported this movement from around the world. Some came to Ferguson to lend support and guidance, and others made handsome financial contributions. While all of these actions have supported the aims of the movement, this book is limited in scope to the perspectives of a few dozen clergy who live and work in the St. Louis area. These on-the-ground perspectives are not intended to diminish or minimize other perspectives; rather, they are presented to orient the reader to the context of this movement within the wider St. Louis area.

I interviewed 24 local faith leaders who are deeply connected to the faith community in St. Louis, and are affiliated with a range of mainline denominations that include the African Methodist Episcopal Church, Roman Catholic Church, Christian Church (Disciples of Christ), Episcopal Church, National Baptist Convention, Inc., Presbyterian Church (USA), United Church of Christ, United Methodist Church, and Unitarian Universalist. I also interviewed a Jewish rabbi and two Protestant clergy affiliated with a nondenominational church. I interviewed an equal number (12) of women and men, 11 of them black and 13 white, with an average age of 47. Three identified themselves as gay or lesbian. I asked open-ended questions that encouraged them to tell their stories of how and when they learned about Michael Brown's death, their immediate reactions, what compelled them to subsequent actions, and how they understood the implications of their actions as relating to the mission of the church. I also wanted to get their takes on the most compelling phenomena within this movement: the emergence of young leaders.

Any book that is related to Ferguson events in the wake of Michael Brown's death would be incomplete without the acknowledgment of young leaders and their critical location within the movement.

While that topic alone is worthy of a series of books, I wanted to try to capture a dimension of their presence in relation to clergy. I invited a *few* young leaders whom I knew worked with clergy to share their reflections with me. I interviewed 13 young leaders who represented or worked with the Deaconess Ann House (Episcopal Service Corp), Metropolitan Congregations United, Millennial Activists United, and Tribe X. Nine are women and four are men. Seven are white, five are black, and one is Taiwanese-American. Two identified themselves as gay or lesbian. Their average age is 22.

To be clear: I do not suggest that young leaders emerged within this movement *because* of the clergy. Actually, I think the argument could be made that the *young leaders* ignited the leadership among the clergy; they created space and impetus for the clergy I talked with to live into their roles as leaders. From the early days in August until this very moment, young leaders and clergy have remained vigilant in their commitment to bearing witness to the atrocity of Michael Brown's killing–both in the streets as well as in strategy meetings. Although I have participated in many public actions that included clergy (and congregants) and young leaders, I was curious to learn more about how the two mixed and mingled over the first few months. What were the points of connection and departure? How did they create space to hear and see each other anew? What did they learn about the church and its possibilities for cultivating and supporting emergent young leaders in the church and society? How might these and other queries point us toward the signposts that may reveal new insight on what it means for congregations to engage in transformative social action as they consider critical questions about the nature and mission of the church in these turbulent times?

The book has 10 chapters. The stories in each chapter create portraits of a few key moments in the movement, moments that were integral to the connection between clergy and young leaders, leading us toward reflection on the explicit learnings from these events. It is important to note that this book is not a historical account of Ferguson events in the wake of Michael Brown's death, nor is it a "tell-all" about the "inner workings" of a movement. Perhaps the historians and gossip columnists will take up those tasks. As a practical theologian, I took up the work of looking for evidence of God's tenets of love, justice, faithfulness, and hope, and I wanted to tell and reflect on some of that story using the experiences of a few clergy and young leaders.

Chapter 1, titled *Just Protest This by Prayer!*, explores the stories behind the now familiar photo of clergy kneeling to pray in front of the Ferguson police station.

Chapter 2, *Praying with Their Feet,* recounts some of the stories of the urgent calls from Canfield Green Apartments, and the activity that followed. This chapter also briefly explores the following question: "What has been done?" in relation to the St. Louis region and racial justice movements that resulted in mass public displays of protest.

Chapter 3, *Not Looking Away,* describes an overarching theme of the work because there was an emphasis on seeing and not looking away. It describes and explores stories of some of the early and risky decisions that led to expanded commitments within some congregations.

Chapter 4, *Jesus Is in the Streets!,* describes the stories of young leaders arrested in Ferguson on October 2 and taken to the St. Ann jail, and the role clergy played in support of them. Young leaders also take to task the notion of respectability politics, and its impotence in this movement.

Chapter 5, *Where Have All the Leaders Gone?,* explores the origins of the #BlackLivesMatter movement and highlights the leading role of women in the protests.

Chapter 6, *This Is What Theology Looks Like,* recounts the clergy march on Moral Monday on October 13. The chapter explores the theological and ethical imperatives for this movement.

Chapter 7, *Why Are Your Doors Open to Us?,* reframes the idea of "safe sanctuaries" and casts it through the lens of congregational responses as hosts to the #BlackLivesMatter freedom rides and in the aftermath of the off-duty police shooting death of Vonderrit Myers in South St. Louis City on October 8.

Chapter 8, *There Is a Ferguson Near You,* explores the issue of doing racial justice in communities outside of the immediate Ferguson area.

Chapter 9, *Standing on the Side of Love,* offers a different framework. Instead of taking the prescribed sides, it engages in a reflection on how clergy and young people understood their work as standing on the side of love.

Chapter 10, *#staywoke,* is a critical reflection on what the church needs to do to stay awake to the racial justice issues that have resurfaced, the vision of leadership cast by the young emergent leaders, and the implications for building a beloved community that will lead us into a future filled with hope.

As I reflect on my conversation with parents at the birthday party, I wonder if faith communities and clergy may feel that leaving some of their familiar ways of doing and being church is too big of a step. This may be true, but, if you *do* take some steps, my hope is that this book is a source of encouragement to help you find your footing quickly.

A memorial to Mike Brown at the shooting scene on Canfield Drive in Ferguson. *(Photo by Leah Gunning Francis)*

CHAPTER 1

Just Protest This by Prayer!

"All my life, my political and social and spiritual selves have all moved together; I just could not separate them."

United Methodist Bishop Leontine T. C. Kelly

The Ferguson police station was a daily site for protests after Michael Brown was killed. For months, protestors regularly gathered in front of the police station to bear public witness to their outrage because of the shooting death of Michael Brown. They chanted, marched, and held up signs. They made their demands known to the police through chants such as, "What do we want? Justice! When do we want it? Now!" and they implicated the entire criminal justice system with chants such as, "The whole d**n system is guilty as h**l!" They were resolute in their witness, and were determined to give voice to the egregiousness of this offense. When they chanted, "We're young, we're strong, we're marching all night long," they meant it. They were young, as most were in their late teens and twenties. They were strong, as their fortitude was unwavering in what became for them a daily way of life. And, oftentimes, they marched long into the night.

On September 29, a typical protest night took a memorable turn. Young activists were present and chanting fervently, and the police were posted in front of them, fully dressed in riot gear. However, on this day, more clergy were present than usual, because word had spread that young protestors were often being arrested during these evening protests. In the midst of the standoff, a few clergy took a decidedly different public action: they knelt on the sidewalk outside the police station and prayed. They symbolically laid down their collars on the altar of justice and made clear that their resistance was an action of their faith.

Clergy kneel to pray between police and protesters at the Ferguson police station on September 29. *(Photo by Philip Deitch)*

Many pictures were taken of this action and posted quickly on social media. These pictures were often described as "iconic" because they depicted clergy doing something many had not seen in any Ferguson-related events. Not only did they voice their support of the protestors, but they put their bodies on the line and brought the gravitas of their moral authority to the moment and movement. They sent a clear message that they were bringing the resources and authority of their faith to the cause of racial justice.

Several notable events happened that evening as soon as the clergy knelt to pray. First, the atmosphere changed from raucous and rowdy to silent. The chanting stopped and the protestors listened to the prayer. The police seemed uncertain how to respond, since they were confronted with a different kind of protestor and tactic. Surely someone had to consider what the optics would look like if they dragged the group of middle-aged, collar-wearing, loudly praying clergypeople off the sidewalk and cuffed them. None of the clergy were arrested that night, and it became a mile-marker in the movement for racial justice.

Rebecca Ragland, pastor of Holy Communion Episcopal Church in University City, Missouri, describes her experience from that evening.

I heard on the news that people were getting arrested at the police department. Even by the end of September protestors seemed to say "We're not giving up on this." So I went to Ferguson and there were a lot of clergy. We had emailed a lot of the people we knew and said, "We need to go," and so we went. We were trying to say, "I think we need to be present because there needs to be de-escalation" since there had been this string of arrests every night.

The protestors were doing their thing. It seemed fine, but we didn't really know each other yet, the people that were out on the line. Then we all stepped out into the road, and the cars were still coming, and Mike Kinman and I started to direct traffic with several other people. We were just trying to keep the traffic away so the cars could turn around.

Then the police came forward. There was a little interaction and then it was really scary. Everybody's scared, and then [Osagyefo] Sekou went forward and knelt. Mike was really instrumental in getting the kneeling part for us because we were both just standing there praying out loud and then we came right up onto the sidewalk and we all just knelt. As we knelt then the protestors, who had been in the middle of the street, came forward and stood behind us. And as they did that, it got just quiet. You could actually hear crickets. It was that quiet just for a minute.

Sekou prayed out loud and then I prayed and Mike prayed and so we prayed up and down the line, and I thought to myself, "If we keep praying, we could pray all night and just protest this by prayer."

Jon Stratton, an Episcopal priest and director of the Episcopal Service Corp, was present that night with several of the interns from the service corp. He describes the evening in this way:

So there were about 20 or 30 people, and police come out in their riot gear. There was a row of young protestors in the street. The police were saying, "Get out of the street or we're going to arrest you for unlawful assembly. Disperse or you'll be arrested." And the clergy knelt down in front of the police with the protestors behind, and the atmosphere changed. We knelt down and prayed, and the atmosphere completely changed. The protestors—this is amazing—the young protestors came up behind the clergy, laid their hands on the clergy and knelt as well and prayed.

And it was very tense in the moment right before we knelt down and prayed. The police were dumbfounded when we did that. They didn't know what to do. That was the first time that clergy were out in this way. I mean, there were clergy who were out all the time, so I don't want to discount that. But this was the first time clergy were out in a really visible way, and I think it just surprised the police and changed the atmosphere that night. I mean, there were no arrests made. There was no tear gas or rubber bullets. The police stood down. They eventually left.

The Episcopal Service Corp intern program is a ministry of the Episcopal Church. Through this ministry, recent college graduates commit to one year of service in a designated U.S. city in nonprofit or church-related organizations. Jon Stratton describes the program as

...a national program in the Episcopal Church. There are about 30 different locations of intentional communities, of young adults in their 20s who are taking a year to live in community, together under one roof, to share our common rule of life. It's based on Benedictine values and Benedictine spirituality, and then they work in not-for-profits for that year. So kind of like AmeriCorps meets St. Benedict meets the Episcopal Church, Dorothy Day kind of thing.

This particular cohort began their St. Louis internship over Labor Day weekend; however, they committed to serve for one year in St. Louis before August 9 and quickly found themselves engaged in the Ferguson protests. Seven young adults came to St. Louis from around the country, despite some of their loved ones' fears and discouragement.

Brendan O'Connor, an intern from Wisconsin, describes his rationale for getting involved in the protests:

I felt compelled to go to the things that Jon Stratton had been inviting us to in these protests for a number of reasons. I really had a sense that this is the city and the community that we're entering into. If we want to be serious about this, that we want to be a part of this, and we want to be part of the force that is here to help and stand for just the Christian ideal here in St. Louis, then we have to be a part of this.

It doesn't mean that we get to be the leaders. I never thought of myself as being some sort of leader or on the frontlines, but I recognize that this was a moment where I had to at least be there to listen and to learn and even just be a body for support. And I was there at a number of events, but I was never especially salient. And I can recognize that I'm not like one of the saviors of these events, and I'm okay with that.

I was an auxiliary member of the Student Labor Action Coalition [in college]. So it was, I felt, like a way to add another layer into my trying to understand things about justice, and this was a police-related thing which is something I hadn't had much experience, and also involving race relations. So before [Ferguson], I happened to watch the film "Fruitvale Station," which was about the killing of Oscar Grant. So this seemed pretty real and it was very disconcerting realizing like why does this keep happening, and, also made me mindful that this event and the response to it is not – this isn't a onetime thing. This has happened before.

Rosemary Haynes, an intern from North Carolina, describes her experience that night in front of the police station.

So [September 29] was a Monday, and on Mondays, we have Eucharist, and it's our community meal. And after all that was over, Jon asked us if we would go because we're seen as faith leaders, and he thought that our presence would be welcomed and needed. So I went, and, of course, I was kind of nervous. I mean, coming from the South, people are like, "Don't go over there. It's not safe." But, of course, I went anyway, and I remember getting there and I'd never seen riot police ever before. So it was very shocking to me, but when we got there, there was a line of young adults in the street. And I just remember just being so proud and just like—I just wanted to be one of them. And so we gathered, and we wrote the jail support number on our arms, and that was nerve-racking because I was like, "Oh, my gosh, I'm going to get arrested." We joined in the street, and we were locking arms. And the police called out, "If you're in the street, you're subject to arrest." So I just stood there, and I was just like, "I'm going to do this," like, "I want to do this because how else can I be a part of this without putting myself in the shoes of those young people who have been there since August 9?" So it's what I wanted to do. And so I stood there and then clergy walked up. Reverend Sekou walked up first and kneeled down and then Bill Perman and Jon Stratton walked up with him, and they were kneeling, and they were praying. And so myself and my other housemates walked up, and we kneeled behind them.

Many of the young adult interns who were beginning their service in St. Louis wanted to personally experience the same process their peer protestors had been engaged in since August 9. This kind of experiential learning was important to them as they reflected on their experiences and shared with friends whose only perspective was the news. Sherry Nelson, an Episcopal Service Corp intern from Illinois, shares her experience of talking with her family and friends who did not support the movement and trying to give them another perspective of what was actually happening in St. Louis.

I started out like watching Rosemary's involvement, and I had a lot of conversations with people back home that were very much in disagreement with like me supporting the movement, Black Lives Matter, and like everything going on. And so I started out in that way, just having a lot of conversations with her and bouncing ideas off of her of ways to help people view things differently and things like that and then I started joining her on the streets in protests and Rebecca [Ragland] too.

And, before that, I was just going to a lot of educational things like events at churches and things like that but then I realized like, okay, this is not stopping. I want to get more involved in another way and I'm being way too comfortable in the way that I am approaching this. It's time to get out of the box. So I stepped into the streets and started protesting and it was nerve-racking, but it made a huge difference in my life. I've learned a lot through the time that we've spent here, and I'm excited to continue to be involved.

Tori Dahl, an intern from Minnesota, describes her experience that evening. For Tori, one of the greatest values of her participation was to be able to tell others what was really happening on the ground, sharing an account that was different from media reports. From her perspective, the media mostly reported from a particular lens that often shone a negative spotlight on the protestors.

So Jon [Stratton] just said, "I think this is really important, and I would love to have you come out and add to our clergy numbers because we've been asked to support this cause. And it would mean a lot to me, and I think it's important, but, of course, it's your decision." And so I was nervous but also did feel a call to be involved and to see what was going on and to be able to be a voice back, and I think that's maybe been the biggest thing, at least for me, but maybe for others too—to talk to people from home and from other places and to say that, yes, this is being skewed, and there's so much peaceful and positive things happening.

One of the peaceful moments Tori described was during the time when the clergy kneeled to pray. This is significant because peace did not equate silence; peace emerged in a way that gave voice to the angst and suffering of those who fought for justice.

The most powerful thing for me was that we were in the middle of this really raucous crowd and it had gotten kind of scary, and they were ready to head out. But the clergy stepped out, kneeled down to pray, and it just went silent. And there was just like this really powerful moment of peace, and the police didn't know what to do. I think, at that point, they may have even walked away because this crowd that had been chanting and loud had just entirely gone silent and was listening to Reverend Sekou pray, and that was one of the most powerful moments for me that night.

For several who were present that night, the presence and prayers of clergy were not merely *symbolic* of God's presence, but they report *feeling* the presence of God. The public witness of clergy symbolizing the presence of God was made known. Rosemary Haynes continued her reflection by talking about how that moment made God's presence tangible for her.

That moment of prayer was like the first time that I really felt God. Well, I've never been like super religious. I've always been more spiritual. Like I just felt God's presence and meaning that, in that moment, I knew that I was supposed to be there, and I was seeing God in all the people who were there which I had never, like, experienced that before. So that night has had pretty much everything to do with my faith and where I am now.

Like most pictures, there is a story behind the now-familiar photo that rarely gets unearthed. The photo of the clergy kneeling only captures one part of what happened that evening. A glaring question that many observers had was, "What happened after they prayed? What happened after they got up off their knees?" Jon Stratton describes the way that the young activists asserted themselves as leaders, and the clergy offered support from the sidelines.

After the prayer, we got up, and we asked the young folks, "Do you want us to stand in the street with you now that we've done this?" And they said, "No. We appreciate your support, but this is our thing now." And the clergy went to the sidewalk and just prayed on the sidelines, supported, but we took our cues—that night, anyway—from the young folks, particularly the Millennial Activists United. They were kind of calling the shots that evening.

David Gerth is the executive director of Metropolitan Congregations United (MCU), an interfaith coalition of congregations working for social change. He was instrumental in engaging clergy in the protests. He also talks about what happened after the prayer, and how he recognized the spirit of God at work.

So that prayer moment was pivotal, but what was more pivotal—for me—was as that started to break up, there were 16 or 17 protestors, most were Millenial Activists that stood on the center line of the street, locked arms, and they began chanting. And they were disciplining other protestors, you know: "You're in or you're out." And I don't remember what all was said, but it was the first time that I could see that there was a discipline and a direction and some very clear goals. And I thought, "Oh, maybe there are some clergy that I could bring to this because, if they'd see this, they might not want to do it, but they would respect what's going on here." And, theologically, for me, it was that night, when I watched them, and the image for me is that their feet drilled into the core of the earth and they were pulling out raw magma. I mean it was—it's just his level of power. And I know that's not exactly a theological image, but, for me, then I recognized, "The spirit of God is in this place. Whether they're claiming it or not, I'm claiming it." And so, then I knew my job was to figure out whom I could get up, just even if they came for 45 minutes just to watch. You need to see this firsthand because this is not what you have been reading and watching. There is something different going on here, and it's powerful.

Many clergy saw themselves as witnesses to a truth that was not being portrayed in the media, and were compelled to tell others the truth about what they'd seen and heard. This was a clarion call to come and see the power of God at work through the young activists. The media has portrayed them as rebel-rousing looters, but the clergy bearing witness to their actions saw something very different. Yes, there were some people who took advantage of the mayhem and looted stores and business. However, they were not representative of the people at the heart of this movement. They were not the same people holding vigil in front of the Ferguson police station, marching along the St. Louis area streets, rallying at the County Prosecutor's office day after day demanding justice on behalf of Michael Brown. They were not the same people who strategized and organized with local and national groups for the cause of racial justice and human freedom. The young activists represented the heart of this movement. They embodied the courage, strength, and fortitude that inspired the winds of justice to blow across the country and call people to consciousness about the racial injustice sanctioned by the state against black bodies.

For the clergy, standing up for justice on behalf of Michael Brown was about joining the work of God in the world. This was a tipping point in the fight against black lives being deemed as disposable. The people I interviewed, and many more, heeded the call of God to call for justice on behalf of Michael Brown and all black bodies that are deemed less than human. This movement has beckoned all of us to see black people as human beings created in the *imago Dei*—the image of God.

Prayer is a common link to most expressions of faith, but the question this prayer moment raises for us is: "What happens after we pray? What do we actually do in response to that for which we have prayed?"

CHAPTER 2

Praying with Their Feet

"I prayed for 20 years but received no answer until I prayed with my legs."

Frederick Douglass

Shortly after Michael Brown was killed, social media lit up with images of his body lying in the middle of Canfield Drive. Since this street is the main thoroughfare through the apartment community, the scene could be viewed from many different vantage points. Brown's body laid bare for the entire community to see as cries of grief emerged from his family and friends. As word spread about his death, more people began to gather at the scene. While there was a range of responses, in this chapter we hear a few stories about some of the clergy actions in the immediate hours and days following Brown's death.

Many different factors influenced their decision to respond. Some were in close physical proximity to Canfield Drive or were personally asked to respond in some way. Others were faced with a moral and ethical dilemma that demanded their attention, or had personally experienced racial profiling. For most, it was a combination of these factors, among others. But a crucial factor that seemed to frame every decision was a vocational matter—that they were called or inspired by God to do this work. This work was informed by their faith, and expressed in a variety of ways.

For Such a Time as This

In the biblical story of Esther, she finds herself challenged by her cousin Mordecai to use her royal status and influence, born of a forced sexual relationship with the king, to thwart Haman's plan to have all of the Jewish people killed. Esther was orphaned as a child and raised by her cousin Mordecai. When she was summoned by King Xerxes and made his queen, she neglected to mention she was Jewish because her cousin Mordecai instructed her to keep it a secret. Then, at the critical moment, Mordecai implored Esther to use her privilege to act on behalf of the Jewish people. Mordecai's final plea to Esther struck a tone that has resonated with people of faith for centuries when he said, "And who knows but that you have come to royal position for such a time as this?" This story is often cited to call people to reflect on their own purpose when discerning how their position can constructively be used for the benefit of others when faced with moral or ethical dilemmas.

Some variation of "for such a time of this" came up repeatedly in the interviews for this book. Several clergy reported feeling called to respond in the ways that they did. They connected it with a greater purpose and described how God seemed to use their life skills, experiences, and resources for the benefit of this collective effort. In this chapter, four clergy reflect on their responses to the killing of Michael Brown, Jr. Willis Johnson is the pastor of Wellspring United Methodist Church, a predominately African American congregation in Ferguson. He begins by discussing the way he leveraged his proximity to try to mediate tense situations between the police and protestors.

I don't live too far from the Ferguson police station. Not only did I see the Facebook postings and hear about it, but also I literally heard the voices and the demonstration of the young people on August 9. That evening, I walked to the corner and saw people gathering. Then I told my wife, "I'm going to go down towards the police station and check this out." And, from that point on, for about three hours, I stayed there with young people who were obviously upset, frustrated, and angered. The group of young people wanted to get some answers, and they were really going to rush the police station. And I'm sure I was not the only person there that said, "Well, maybe that's not the best of ideas." I started talking to someone who's since become a voice in the movement, Tory Russell. He was one of the young men out there who had kind of been conversing with the Brown family and some other people, I think. I said to him and some others, "I live here. I pastor the church down the street. Not that I'm important but I think maybe I can go [into the police station]. Because, if you all go over here now, they're not going to respond well," and not to mention the facility was under construction, renovation. So they had an alternative way to get in, and it was just not, in my opinion, going to be well received if a group of people kind of converged.

They buzzed me into the police station because somebody at the front desk knew who I was. And I said, "Hey, I know this is a very, very tense situation and you all have a group of folk out here who are demanding answers. They're not going to leave until they talk to somebody, and I know about the curfew. I know you probably can't talk to them. But is there any way I can talk to somebody here and explain the situation?" So they got me the captain on duty. He came out with about three or four other officers, and I, again, went through the formality, saying who I was. I live here, pastor there, and I know the situation. The first thing, he's like, "Well, we can't talk to anybody. We just can't." I said, "Sir, I understand, but if you want to have some resolve this evening and just get to the next day, can you at least talk to them for a moment? Even saying that 'I can't say anything' is at least saying something."

So they agreed to that. I went back across the street said, "Hey, I'm going to bring three or four folk to talk to the police. You all choose who the three or four folks will be." And somebody came and they were recording, and we walked back across the street. They asked a few questions at that time. Of course, none of them could get answered. They wanted some specific details. We spent about five, seven minutes going back and forth, and they were at least able to see, physically, that they got to talk somebody. They obviously told the rest of the group, probably a hundred or so folks. I remember going home a little bit after midnight and, for the most part, the crowd had dissipated. However, they said they'd be back, and they were.

I got up early that Sunday morning. I usually run on Sundays and, as I was doing my route on South Florissant, I could already see TV trucks coming in, local stations preparing and organizing in the police department next to the firehouse. I asked a reporter,

"What's going on?" He said, "Well, there's supposed to be a press conference this morning." So I shortened my run, got dressed, and got into the press conference that was actually supposed to be closed. There were a few elected officials there that day like Antonio French. There was a group that was out there led by local activist Anthony Shahid; he and some other folks began to gather early on. That Sunday really began the protests— the prolonged protests that most of us are accustomed to seeing. And it was the first Sunday that I began to address this communal concern from the pulpit.

In addition to levering his proximity and community status to mediate between police and protestors, he also attended to the impact of his church's close location to the police station. He chose to engage the congregation in conversation about the theological imperative to doing this work, and the need to engage people who may not be a part of the church.

Our church is less than .3 miles from the [Ferguson] police station so it had to be addressed... You could hear the activity inside our church. I talked about how the church needed to respond, and that we need to hear the voices that come from the outside. And I talked about how this was not a time to be quiet. It was not a time to quibble, and it was not a time to quit. I think this is what Mordecai challenges Esther with, that for—in some shape, form, or fashion—we are positioned and we need to present ourselves ready for such a time as this.

Many of our congregants live here. They were going to see the newscasts. They were going to hear, and have continuously heard the chants, and they had to wrestle with the question of whether they would demonstrate in some type of way. And so I thought it was imperative to be able to give them some theological grounding that was sound and that was within our tradition of both faith and practice. I believe that Jesus was a radical, a revolutionary. He was demanding systematic change. And a lot of what Jesus said was provocative and yet prophetic. So I went from not only comforting and challenging my existing congregation but, then, because we opened the doors of our church, we were becoming an epicenter for activity. We were spurring or welcoming dialogue and housing constituencies that were outside not only our faith tradition but also even some of the culture demographic. I felt it was imperative to speak to that but to honor the faith tradition, and so we went from not only wrestling with questions internally about, "How do we participate as Christians?" but then said to those who are outside of the church, "You know what, we're not the enemy. We may not speak in the same way but the spirit of what you're saying resonates. It aligns."

And so, yes, black lives do matter, and yes, they matter because there's a God who believes that all life is sacred. While this has racial implications and tension and economic reverberation, there's a historical record of a system and a culture that are violent toward black people at any given time, and the design of the system and the practice of the culture is not non-discriminate. When it gets through with one, it goes to the other. So there is a God who is a God of all the oppressed. There's a God who cares, and there's a sacredness of person because we're all created in the image of God.

We Need You To Do Something!

Every now and then, people you do not know may recognize your work. This was the case for Traci Blackmon when she received her first request to "do something" after Michael Brown was killed. Traci is the pastor of Christ the King United Church of Christ in Florissant, Missouri. She is the first woman pastor in the church's 159-years-long history and continues her bi-vocational work as pastor and as a coordinator for faith-based initiatives for a local hospital system.

I learned of his death over social media. I was perusing Facebook, and I got a private message from someone whom I did not know that well but apparently knew me and called me by "Pastor Traci" and told me that a young man had been killed in Canfield. And I wasn't even really sure where Canfield was at the time. She attached a photo of the yellow tape and the body laying in the middle of the street. And so, I began to see it as the attention grew higher and higher around it and began to trend all over Facebook as I was watching the conversation. That was on August 9. Her original request of me was, "We need you to do something." And I didn't respond to her immediately because I didn't know what I could do. I didn't know the situation. I didn't know anything except that this body was dead, lying in the street. And, to be honest with you, dead bodies are not that unusual in St. Louis or in any of our metropolitan areas. And so, while it saddened me, I didn't exactly understand what it is she thought that I could do about it...and I didn't do much that night except pray and watch what was happening.

As the night got later and later, a lot of my friends of faith were beginning to comment on it, but comments varied. All of them were grief stricken and sad about, "Here we go again." But most of them were leading in the direction of, "Let's pray about this." Or some people said, "Let's wait and see what the circumstances are, what really happened." And as I was watching and reading the different kinds of posts, I put up a post that, really, I said, just rather flippantly, "Well, if all we're going to do is wait and pray, can we at least do that at the police station?" And I got immediate responses saying, "When? What time? What day?" And so just really, as a response to that, I said, "Let's meet there after worship tomorrow. Let's give everyone a chance to get out of worship, and we'll meet there at 3:00." And I asked people to wear their clergy garments and to spread the word.

Traci describes her "God moments," or how she saw God at work, in the following days. She responded to the call, and people responded to her call to participate. She pointed out that she is the pastor of a modest-sized church, and a woman in a community context that is often ambivalent, at best, toward women pastors. These "God moments" she names, pointing to the work of God to bring diverse people together for a common cause.

I had a God moment at the police station, and I experienced one two days later when we gathered at Christ the King for the first time. I didn't know what it meant, but I knew it was a God moment. First of all, the clarion calls to the clergy said, "Spread the word." I was surprised, because I pastor a church of 140 people, and that's 140 on the rolls, because we don't pad the rolls. We clean them out, so…maybe 70 to 80 people on a Sunday morning, so it's not a large church at all even though I have a large building, and I'm a woman who preaches in heels. So I live in a patriarchal region in terms of preaching and in terms of pulpits. My reach is not as great, even with 140…that is not a huge congregation in the first place.

And so I had a God moment when I got to by the police station and I saw all these clergy, and I saw clergy of multiple faiths. So to watch the Nation of Islam stop the traffic and file across as they do and to hold the line, and to see white clergy from different denominations in a place where we are largely segregated on Sunday mornings, and to see black clergy from all different kinds of denominations come out to be a part of this, to see gay clergy come out and to be arm in arm with very extreme conservative clergy… I'm watching God do this. It's a God moment, and there were certain people I had asked to speak because I wanted a wide representation of clergy. But, as it unfolded, there were places where God allowed me to plug in people that I did not know personally but who represented other faiths. So to be able to ask one of our Muslim brothers, "Will you join us and say a prayer?" and to ask one of my gay colleagues, "Will you join us and say a prayer?"; to have seminary representation there and say, "Will you join us and say a prayer?" I recognized it as a God moment. But I did not know what it meant to have all of these young people surrounding us and see us in this moment, in this sacred moment in the midst of our pain, put aside our differences to come and pray.

And I wish that I had stayed in that God moment and paid attention really closely because the clergy part, I got. The youth part was disconnected. The young people, because there were many young people out there, many who are church-raised, for lack of a better word, and many who, perhaps, were raised in the church and had left the church and perhaps even some who had never been to church. They were hurting. They were in pain, and there's a story in the Bible where Jesus goes into the synagogue, and he's teaching. And a woman comes in, who's bent over, and she's been bent over for 18 years [Lk. 13:10–17]. It's the sermon that made T.D. Jakes famous: *"Woman, thou art loosed."* But what intrigues me about that sermon is that the Bible says that she was on the outskirts of the synagogue, and this particular time, Jesus sees her while he's teaching. He sees her bent over, and she's so far bent over. The Bible says that she can't even look up, so all she can see is the ground. For whatever reason, the Bible says that it's a spirit that has her bent over. It doesn't name any kind of infirmity, but in that particular text, this is one time when Jesus—the text says that Jesus sees the woman and calls her to him. And I've always questioned that text. I said, "If there was ever a time for Jesus to go, that was it. You know? *She* made her way into the temple. *She's* obviously ostracized. *She* has this *illness. She's female. She's* in the synagogue, and *she* made her way there. If there's any time that Jesus should make his way over to the—to somebody—this is it.

But he doesn't. He calls for her to come to him, which, if you're bent over and you can't see anything but the ground and all these other people are around you, how intimidating that must be. And so I asked of that text and I asked of the Lord, "Why would you make her come to you? Why wouldn't you go to her? Aren't we called to go to her?" And I just feel that very strongly. Since I've asked that question, I feel it in my spirit that the Lord was saying in that moment that this was not just a moment about her, but it was a moment about communities of worship and that there must be space made in the center of worship for the pain of people. And so, had he gone to the outskirts that space would never have opened up. So if you read that text, the Bible says that Jesus says to her, while she is coming, Jesus says to her, "Woman, you are loosed." He doesn't wait until he touches her, because the reintegration into the center of worship frees her.

So what does that have to do with Michael Brown? I missed the opportunity to call young people. I missed the opportunity to call young people to the center of worship. I missed the opportunity to draw that pain into that healing place. So it was a God moment that was not fully recognized because, in the midst of all of that, I got caught up in the message and forgot the ministry. So it was a powerful moment that people talk about all the time, but it also was a painful moment for me. So the young people listened to the prayers and listened for a long time, but they were hurting. They were hurting. They began to go out in the street and sit in the street. And I asked for them to—I had the bullhorn, and I asked for them to get out of the street, and I asked for them to get out of the street from my mother place not because I thought they were wrong but because I was looking at these policemen, and I didn't want them to be hurt. In their anger and in their pain, I didn't want them to be hurt. So that was a God moment. God continued— as God does—even when you mess up, God continues to work. And so there were lots of God moments that day.

And so one of the things that the Lord had put in my spirit, before the prayer vigil, was to just make a petition. And I didn't know exactly what I was doing, but I just asked for—I think it was five very succinct things: "We want a swift investigation. We want a balanced and impartial decision. We want respect for our communities…" It was just things like that, and I brought it out there and asked people to sign it. And, by the time we went in to see the mayor, it had over 500 signatures on it just from this prayer vigil. And so, in that meeting with him, he was very responsive and apologetic in some ways. Not apologetic for what had happened because he, too, was saying he didn't know the details yet, but he was apologetic for this moment that was happening. And he promised those things, and I said, "Well, since you want to work with us, would you be agreeable to attending a town hall meeting?" And he said, "Yes." Now, at the time I asked him that, I didn't have a town hall meeting. I just said it. I hadn't planned it… It was a God moment. I had not planned a town hall meeting. I just said it, and I said, "And I'd like to present you with this petition from the community." So I gave him that. He agreed, in front of everybody, to come to this town hall meeting, and I said, "On Tuesday," because I knew I hadn't planned anything, and Monday was a little bit too fast.

On Monday, I went to an NAACP meeting at [Murchison Tabernacle CME Church]. I got in, which was another God moment because so many people didn't get in, and I sat there and listened to sermon after sermon and different points of view by lots of people who know lots of things, but there was no plan. And then, when it was time for question and answer, the time had been spent so much in these speeches there was no real time for questions and answers, and the community was angrier. They got shut down, and it was really bad.

So I got to ask a question, which was the next God moment. And I asked, point blank, "We've listened to what you had to say, but you haven't told us what we're going to do. And where is the plan?" And the truth is they didn't have one. None of us had one. So I said, "We're having a town hall meeting tomorrow." Then I knew it had to happen. I didn't have to have the answers. We, collectively as clergy, didn't have to have the answers, but we did need to have a way that people could plug in in such a way that they could discharge some of this anger and energy. They had to have points of discharge.

Town Hall Meeting at Christ the King UCC on August 12

The town hall meeting had to be structured in a way that they could see themselves getting involved, and with different avenues to get involved, so I structured the meeting that way. I've done a lot of facilitation work. I used to do diversity training, so I deal with that energy quite well and I knew that there were certain things that had to be in place. One had to be, in order to control—and not control as in "corral," but in order to... Let me put it this way: I didn't have to control the people, but I had to have my hand on the pressure valve.

There used to be these pots called pressure cookers. And sometimes, when your parents were in a hurry, they would cook something in the pressure cooker because it didn't take as long to cook, but they were very dangerous because, if you didn't have the lid on just right and if you didn't release it just right, the steam would make the lid explode off of the pressure cooker. So what I'm saying is I had to have my finger on the lid, and I had to make sure that there was built into that first meeting enough valves to release pressure, so that people could hear and that we could have a dialogue and that we could do some action planning. I didn't have to have the plan. To have the plan would have been a mistake. But I had to have my hand on that pressure valve. There were things that intentionally built into that. There was a panel, and it was the mayor and the police chief and the head of the Clergy Coalition and the heads of some other prominent faith groups that were in St. Louis because I didn't want anybody to be excluded. And, on my way to the church, I got a call from the governor's office. He heard that I was having this meeting, and he wanted to come and so we had conversation about that, and the governor ended up coming. We had conversation about that because there are benefits to not being the big church and not being the name everybody calls because I didn't have anything to lose. A part of my conversation with his office was, "He can come, but he can't do a stump speech and leave. If that's what he wants to do, he can't come." I said he has to listen. He can speak. Doesn't have to stay the whole time. He's the governor, but he does have to listen. And he was more willing to do that. I had never met Governor Nixon before. So that was my first encounter with him.

So all these people ended up coming to this meeting, and I said to them—and I kept my promise—because, after Monday, everybody was gun shy. I said, "There will not be any verbal attacks here. There's going to be anger because there's anger in this situation, but everybody is going to be respectful and everyone's going to be heard." I set it up so that they got to talk, and so the community knew that they would get to talk. And between them talking and the community, another God moment, I said, "I need someone who can speak well and succinctly and unashamedly about what it means to live in this America as a black person, and I need the community to hear these people saying it. I need the community to see these people hearing it, our legislators, and our government. They need to hear it, but I need someone who can say it without the rage."

So I asked for volunteers. And we had a black man and woman, and the whole purpose was just to tell what it was like for them to raise a black son in St. Louis. I knew what that story was, because I have two black sons and I have a black daughter. I know it very well. Then we had a young man, a teenager, telling his story. So the people who were supposed to be there were there, and the fact that the community could hear somebody speak their truth to the powers that be and could watch the powers that be—and I'm not demonizing the people who were on the stage; I'm speaking of the positions that they held—and watch them listen let off enough pressure. When it was time for the community to speak, they had space because that pressure had been relieved. There were some people who didn't like it because it was too controlled for them, but you're always going to have that. But I think that people left sad, left hurting, left angry, all the emotions they should leave with, but they left with the feeling that, "We can make a difference and we can do something," and thats what I was after.

I Said, "Yes" One Time

Tommie Pierson is the pastor of Greater St. Mark Family Church in Ferguson and a State Representative. Greater St. Mark is less than two miles from the Canfield apartments and quickly became a hub for meetings, press conferences, and rallies shortly after Brown was killed.

I learned about his killing right after it happened. As a matter of fact, I was right here in this room having a meeting, and one of the people in the meeting was Dellwood Mayor Jones. And he got a phone call from someone saying that there was a killing in his city. He called his chief, and his chief informed him that it was not in his city but it was in Ferguson, and so we continued with our meeting. And so, when the meeting was over and I left, going home down Chambers I noticed this long line of cars following this tow truck, this flatbed tow truck with a police car being carried on the back. And people were just following that car, so I'm thinking in my mind this must be something big going on around here with all of these people following this car. And I saw the news and then that's when I realized that this was no ordinary police shooting.

I got a phone call from one of the attorneys who asked could they hold a rally here that Tuesday night, and I said yes. And all of the players, Anthony Gray, Attorney Crump, Al Sharpton—the whole local and national crew—were here. And then there were so many people here that they couldn't get inside. And, right after that, people started calling, wanting to have a meeting at the church. They wanted to have a meeting, and it was one after the other, sometimes two or three a day. And then I started getting phone calls from around the world, and they wanted to interview me, and, "How did the church get involved?" and this, that, and the other.

And this thing just kind of blossomed. I got to church one Sunday, and there was a flyer on my windshield, and it was talking about a meeting. And I looked at it, and I said, "Wow. This looks pretty good. I think I'm going to try to go to this." And I turned it over, and it was at this church. [laughs] And during that time, there were people all over the place. We had meetings up in the sanctuary, meetings at the school, meetings back here, meetings downstairs. We were meeting all over the place, and the mayor of Ferguson—we had a meeting with him downstairs; had a bunch of clergypeople. And so that's how I got involved. I said, "Yes" one time.

And that "yes" turned into all of this, and I didn't know what I said yes to; I'll be honest, I had no idea this was going to grow into this, and I understand they had called several of the churches and they had told them no, but I didn't know that at the time. I just said yes because I hardly ever turn anybody away. I don't think I've ever turned anybody away. Not just for this incident but for any reason. We're just kind of an open church, you know.

A couple of Sundays, we had CNN and MSNBC and a whole lot of news, and they taped the whole service. And so we were all kind of trying to find our way and I guess I was the most nervous one of all because I'm standing before all these cameras, and I'd never done it before in my life. So we were trying to figure out how I should handle myself and how to handle all of this fame, if you will, and I think the church handled it pretty well.

Over the years, I've been asked that question: "How do you balance church and politics?" Well, first of all, I don't see myself as a politician. I see myself as a man of faith who happens to politick. Everybody politicks, and ones who don't come up on the short end of the stick. The role of a pastor is to help people, and the role of an elected official is the same: to help people, and so one role helps people on a local level, and the other one helps them on a statewide level. And so I always say I don't have a problem because I just do the same thing I do. I speak up for folk here, and I speak up for folk there, and that's just how we roll.

It Could Have Been Any of Us

Carlton Lee founded The Flood Christian Church in Ferguson in March 2013. Michael Brown, Sr., is a member of this church, where he married his wife Calvina three weeks before Michael Brown, Jr., was killed. Lee learned of Michael's death on Saturday afternoon, and tried to reach out to the family to comfort and pray with them.

I grew up in Ferguson and pastor a church there. After three services on Sunday [August 10] I went home and crashed. About 11:00 at night my cousin called me from Greensboro, North Carolina, and said, "Your city is on fire. Are you guys okay?" I'm like, "My city is not on fire. What are you talking about?" She said, "No. It's on fire." So I roll over, grab the remote, turned onto the news, and saw what was happening. I said, "Okay. Let me get up."

At that time, it was just a standoff between protestors and police. I got up, and headed on down there. When I got into Ferguson, I noticed that the QuikTrip was getting ready to be set on fire. People were in there, and they were getting ready to douse the place and set it on fire. And so, when that happened, we just sat there and we watched it burn. We saw police go crazy. They were swinging their batons and dogs were coming out because they divided the crowd up.

My church is on the other side of Lucas and Hunt [Road in Ferguson]. So I went over toward the side where my church is at, get there. It's probably about 2,000, maybe 3,000, people stuck right there on that side of West Florissant. We heard about all the looting that was taking place, but on my side of West Florissant, nothing had taken place. So people were standing in front of the church and they were asking me, "Pastor, what are we going to do? They have killed a young man and have beat however many people they have beat today. What are we going to do?" I said, "I'm going to go up, and I'm going to talk to them." I had on gym shorts and a white T-shirt, and so I walked up and I talked to one of the police and I said, "Hey, listen. I'm the pastor down the street here. What can I do to help?" The police officer comes in a little bit closer to me, has this dog barking at me, and he says, "You can get the f--- out of here." I said, "I'm not going to leave all these people here." I said, "What can I do realistically?" He said, "Get the f--- out of here." I said, "I'm not going to leave." So he starts screaming at me and he lifts his gun up, puts his gun into my face.

When he saw that the crowd started rushing, I asked the commanding officer—I said, "Can you please ask him to remove his gun from out of my face, because he's causing riffraff now." And so they moved him out of the frontline, put someone else up on the frontline. The captain came to me, or the commanding officer came to me, and said, "Hey, pastor, can you please ask everyone to scoot back?" I talked to the people. Everyone took five steps back. The police took about six steps forward. I said, "I"m not going to keep pushing them back and you guys keep coming forward. We"re not going to do that. Your guys stand still, and I'll ask the protestors to scoot back." So by that time, the protestors did not want to move. So we're literally—the only thing that's dividing police and the protestors was myself. Someone took a picture from my church, and it looked as if I had wasted Kool-Aid on my T-shirt because they had that many red dots on me...but the crowd was listening to me.

Monday was the press conference and I was there with the family and ripping and running and meetings and rallies and all that stuff is getting ready to take place. The Brown family reached out to National Action Network and said, "Can you guys help us out?" And Rev [Al Sharpton] got involved. They called me and said, "Hey, listen. We need some help. This is what's going on." I said, "Yeah. I know." In August, [National Action Network] called for an impartial investigation from outside sources. We called for the federal government to come in and get involved in the civil rights violations of Michael Brown, Jr. We urged to have McCulloch… recuse himself. We called for Governor Jay Nixon to recuse him or remove him and appoint a special prosecutor. In private meetings, we were promised one thing. In public conversation, we were told another.

That [Monday] night, I went back down on West Florissant. When I get there, I hear this loud siren that went off. I didn't know what it was about and saw the police putting on masks. Didn't know what that was about. Saw everybody start taking a couple of steps back. We got shot with tear gas. We got shot with the tear gas first, and, as everyone's trying to run, we're all gagging. We're coughing. We get shot with the rubber bullets… I got hit in the back of the leg with a rubber bullet, and I played paintball, but those hurt a lot harder than paintballs, those rubber bullets. So we got hit with those things.

I was acting as a bridge, if you would, trying to hold the hands of the protestors while yet holding the hands of the police and saying, "What's our common ground?" However, I noticed it was only going to be a handful of police that you can discuss this with. You had a handful of protestors that you can discuss it with. But, for the most part, neither side wanted to listen. Some said, "We're not here to negotiate with them." Others said, "No. We need to have serious conversations with them." Some said, "No. We don't need to talk to them. They are consistently killing us, so we're done talking to them. We are not going to say anything else to these people," and then there were some who completely disagreed. So it was kind of like 50–50.

My work continued, as I'm still the pastor of Michael Brown, Sr., and his family. So it hasn't ended, it doesn't end. And I keep doing this work because I have two brothers, two sons that Michael Brown, Jr., could have been… It could have been any of us. So I wanted to be on the frontline to make sure that this doesn't happen again.

All four of these pastors were among the early and sustained responders in Ferguson. Whether they were asked to respond or saw a need and jumped right in, they each brought the resources of their faith traditions, personal skill sets, and compassionate hearts to provide their own forms of leadership in distinct ways.

Anthony Shahid at 7 a.m. on August 10 outside the Ferguson police station. (*Photo by J.B. Forbes*/St. Louis Post-Dispatch/*Polaris*)

Rally at Greater St. Mark Family Church. *(Photo by Mark Buckner)*

Al Sharpton preaches at the Flood Church (Carlton Lee) after the church building was burned down on November 24. Michael Brown, Sr., and his wife, Carletta, are seated in the front row. Carlton Lee is seated on the right side, front row. *(REUTERS/Adrees Latif)*

CHAPTER 3

Not Looking Away

"Once you see it, you can't unsee it. And once you've seen it, keeping quiet, saying nothing, becomes as political an act as speaking out."

Arundhati Roy

As a practical theologian, one of the tasks I regularly engage students in is making the connection between their life experiences and their current worldviews. I challenge them to think critically about the roles their family histories, ecclesial formations, and social contexts played in shaping the way they see and understand the world around them. This is a critical task in the theologically reflective process because it pushes them to consider the reality that they were not necessarily "born" this way—that is, their understandings about God, church, community, etc., were formed in particular ways through their experiences. Critical theological reflection calls us to examine the contours of our formation and pushes us to see God and each other anew.

In this chapter, four pastors offer reflections on their personal histories, the congregation's history, or St. Louis's protest history. Mary Gene Boteler, pastor of Second Presbyterian Church (USA) in the Central West End neighborhood of St. Louis, tells the first story.

I Am a Child of the Civil Rights Movement

When Michael Brown was killed, Mary Gene had just returned from vacation. While on vacation, she read a book titled *Men We Reaped* by Jesmyn Ward, which is a memoir about the author's experience growing up in rural Mississippi and reflected on five deaths of young black men who were close to her. Although the circumstances of these young men's deaths differed, the connection between their lived experiences in a culture of racism, poverty, and oppression led the author to reflect on the underlying threads that wove their stories together.

I normally write weekly e-pistles to the congregation. In mid to late August I wrote three, which dealt with the situation in Ferguson. Following the tragedy, I wrote, "The news from Ferguson is tragic and heartbreaking. Another unarmed, young, black male has been killed." While on vacation I had read Jesmyn Ward's memoir, *Men We Reaped*. Her book connected the deaths of the young black men in her life with the history of racism and the resulting economic struggle, and so I was able to quickly frame the present situation and talk about the anger of the community and address the burning of buildings as an act, while not supporting, we need to understand the underlying reasons.

A congregant wrote to thank me for the e-pistle: "I can only imagine that his immediate and extended families are devastated by this horrible mistake." That word—*mistake*—I had to address the use of the word *mistake*; I couldn't let it hang there. I wrote another e-pistle in which I addressed the inadequacy of the word *mistake*. It didn't rise to the horrific level of the act perpetrated by the officer who shot Michael Brown. He may have not even been aware of what he was doing, but it's like this whole history of racism and the prejudice that had been nurtured in him came out in the finger that pulled the trigger.

I am a child of the first Civil Rights Movement. I was in elementary school during that time and I have...there are stories. My entire life has been shaped in a powerful way by being a child in the '60s in Grenada, Mississippi. Grenada sits along Highway 51 between Memphis and Jackson. When Martin Luther King, Jr., took up James Meredith's march in 1966 after Meredith was shot, he walked right through our place, along our cotton fields. My brothers, who were working in the fields, remember seeing him. Grenada was a hotbed of activity during that long, hot summer;

the SCLC [Southern Christian Leadership Conference] was firmly ensconced in Grenada while SNCC [Student Nonviolent Coordinating Committee, pronounced "snik"] operated 30 miles west in Greenwood.

My first day of high school was the day the schools were desegregated in Grenada. My mother had warned me, "Go straight to the car after school and wait for your brother." The white children were released from school first and then the black children. From the front seat of our old Rambler, I watched as black children came out of the building and the mob gathered around them and beat the hell out of them with metal pipes and other objects. Tears rolled down my face but I was conflicted about the larger situation. I had been raised in a community that supported the segregation of schools, and yet, this kind of violent response would never have been tolerated in my home. It was a tragic day. Over the years, I wondered if my mind had imagined that first day.

A few years ago I read Charles Bolton's book *The Hardest Deal of All,* in which the first chapter is a reenactment of that first day of desegregation in Grenada. My first thought was, "I didn't make it up. It really did happen as I remembered it." However, it was painful for my adult self to realize what I did not understand as a young person. The entire scene had been orchestrated, with white children protected, and with law enforcement agreeing to stand down as black children were assaulted.

In my family of seven children we were never allowed to use disrespectful language about anyone. The "n" word would not only have been unacceptable but also a cause for punishment. And yet, in our kitchen there were two sinks—one where the maids would wash the family's dishes and one where they would wash their dishes. It is the kind of thing you think back on and wonder, "Oh, my gosh, what did we think we were going to catch?" And these weren't—it's just the way things were.

But the same people who acquiesced to segregation were the same people who taught me about Jesus and welcomed me into the church. They weren't bad people; they were simply the product of their own culture. It took me many years before I could come to terms with the fact that the same elders who carefully removed the white cloth from the elements and served me the sacrament that summer also stood outside the door of the church to inform African Americans that they were not welcomed to worship with us.

I think my pastor, the Rev. Emmett Barfield, was pressured to leave the First Presbyterian Church in Grenada that summer. He accompanied young, black children as they walked to school, which must have angered some in the congregation. I seem to remember that his picture was in the local paper. No one has confirmed that he was asked to leave, but I have been in pastoral ministry long enough to know the signs.

Another pastor, the Rev. Bob Walkup, had a huge influence on me. When I was a young pastor in Auburn, Alabama, and found myself in some hot water, I made a visit to his home. He told me the story of being asked to leave his church in Starkville, Mississippi—of getting in his car and heading out with his family with tears streaming down his face. I responded, "Oh, Bob, I don't know what I would do if a church asked me to leave." He replied, with his gravelly voice, "There are a lot of churches, but you only have one soul. Don't lose it." I have carried those words with me and it has made me pretty fierce. I can honestly say that I have never come close to losing my soul in the pulpit.

There may be some in the congregation who are tired of me talking about Ferguson, but what they ought to understand is that I'm a child of Mississippi. I saw children beaten. I witnessed pastors being thrown out of churches. I really believe, in some way, that God has called me to this church, to this city, and to this place for this moment. After all these years of pastoral ministry, I believe that God has called me to this moment and to this congregation to preach God's uncompromising word when it comes to the systemic racism that permeates every institution in our society—even the church.

The Right Side of History

Heather Arcovitch is the pastor of First Congregational Church of St. Louis (UCC) in Clayton, Missouri. Clayton is the county seat for

St. Louis County, so when protestors chanted, "We're taking the heat to the county seat," they were talking about the protests in front of the St. Louis County Justice Center in Clayton. First Congregational Church is less than two miles from the justice center, and many in the congregation are lawyers and local residents.

I preached a lot in those first few weeks, and I remember, early on, it was about not looking away... This is much more than this one officer and one young man. This is a whole systemic thing that we can't move away from anymore. This is happening and we need to not look away. I remember when I went to my council prior to a PICO [People Improving Communities through Organizing] event, when I realized I might start being quoted in the news or be photographed for news media. And I said, "When I speak, am I speaking—I mean, I have the right to speak by means of my own citizenship, my own ordination. But do I have your permission to speak as the pastor of this church? I know I can't speak for the church, but can I name my affiliation if I'm asked?"

And they were initially very, very positive that this is who we are. This is what we stand for. This congregation is the oldest Protestant church this side of the river, and it was founded by abolitionists. So they started as a Presbyterian Church right before the Civil War and called a man who was in Illinois but was an abolitionist Congregationalist preacher, and he refused and refused. He wouldn't lay his bones down in a slave state, and they convinced him, and he signed a three-year contract...but with the stipulation that he would not stop preaching abolition. And he drew a line in the sand, and they said okay. And, at the end of his contract, he was packing up to leave, and the congregation, independently, called a vote and two-thirds of the congregation voted to become Congregational because that was the denomination that was most involved in the abolition movement for the war, and the other third remained Presbyterian.

And so this church became First Congregational of St. Louis, and that's its history. And then, as the war happened, they were very involved in the antislavery movement. During this time it was illegal to teach people of color to read and so they organized

Bible studies, and they were part of the early church school Bible study movement that was organized to teach black people to read "under the radar." I mean, there are really cool roots there. And, now, the congregation's been part of a lot of activism over the centuries of its history, but it hasn't recently found purchase and so that was part of why they called me. The idea was: "Let's get back involved in social justice. We have this mission and vision, and let's get back involved." So I thought, "Okay, here we go." They affirmed—the council affirmed that, you know. "This is who we are."

And so I had to sort of build that plane as I was flying it, and we're an Open and Affirming congregation. And the congregation went through a two-year process to become O & A and they were very intentional, and they really took a slow pace to bring everyone along. And, in the end, they had a pretty well unanimous vote, and people kept saying to me, "Why can't we do [Ferguson response] like the O & A process? We took our time. That's how we do things." And I kept saying, "Because you didn't have a young gay man burned on the lawn, and there wasn't a moment where you were ignited because of historic events of cruelty or community pain that was so compelling that you couldn't not act. You made an intellectual decision, an emotional decision, a faith-based, and an ethical decision, and then you have the luxury of taking your time. And we don't have that right now.

"Our city's on fire, and I'd like to be on the right side of history, but, also, ethically, we've been awakened, and once you're awakened, you can't look away." You don't agree with everything everybody does. And the nights when I stood out with protestors and looting started, to come back to my congregation and say, "Yes. I was standing there with the looters, and while I don't affirm looting, I have come to understand why violent expressions occur in the midst of this kind of communication." I mean, protest as the language of the unheard is real, and protests— you ignite something. You can't always control how the flames go, but, sometimes, you need to stand there and protect the fire. And it's very difficult and delicate conversation to have, but it's a foundational understanding. And that was a big learning curve for me to try and bring a congregation that really didn't know me along in that conversation, and we're still working on it.

I preached a sermon about our "black lives matter" sign to make it clear where I stood and...the rationale for it being there. I understood that, for some members, as a UCC congregation, we agree to live in disagreement. We agree to be in discernment all the time together. And so I made it very clear in the sermon that I knew that there would be some members that drove in and said, "Yes. This is why I'm a member of this congregation because we stand for justice... We act out of beliefs." But I also knew there would be others who would drive in and say, "Oh, come on. Can we be done with this already?" or, "Why can't it say *all* lives matter?" So we talked about the difference between "black lives matter" and "all lives matter." I'm not entirely certain what all emerged in all its nuances, but people were receptive. They were definitely receptive, and I didn't say anything any more insightful than what everyone's saying about those lines.

And, honestly, for a lot of white people, it's a learned thing. I think, for a lot of black people, it's a learned thing, too. How do I use the language of this movement and what am I obscuring if I use language that isn't fully articulated right, clearly? And so, as a gay clergyperson, I went through a similar process. When you decide whether you're going to come out to your congregation in your search process and your associations, part of that conversation is about when you make it blatant. It's like you're saying you're an instant activist, right? So if I say, "Hi. I'm Heather, and I'm gay...," well, most people don't say, "Hi, I'm Pastor Christina, and I'm straight." So having to say it gives people a little awkwardness. If you didn't have to say it, if they could discern some other way, like, "Here's my partner who also happens to be my same sex, and therefore, you can figure it out," it's less jarring, and there's something about this, too.

There's something about the language that's about its truth. If you say "black lives matter," now you're saying that we haven't been saying that. And, if we haven't been saying that, that makes me feel uncomfortable because you're accusing me of something. And whether I should be accused of that or not, it makes me uncomfortable, and so I can't get to the content because I'm stuck at a front, and I think that's just human nature. But then the other piece is that having to say it, you know, for me, as a gay person, if you're not assuming that anyone could fall anywhere on the sexuality—on the sexual orientation spectrum, then you're assuming that straight is normative. And you don't know it. Most people don't know it. So they don't mean to be exclusionary. They genuinely don't know. So that leaves it to me to have to explain it to advocate for myself—right?— which is difficult. I can pass.

While the gay experience in America and the black experience in America are very different and distinct, there are echoes of similarity. I think that there are large swaths of people who genuinely don't know, haven't been exposed and haven't had to think about it. That is what privilege does... So when they're exposed, some people say, "Oh, my God, that's heartbreaking. I never noticed it before." And some people go, "Oh, hell no. You're not going to accuse me of that." And then some people try and minimize in both of those camps, and so, to keep people from minimizing, to get people into the conversation in a way that they can stay there long enough that maybe some change can happen—maybe some wisdom, maybe some maturity in the way that we think about it can occur—is a really delicate negotiation. And I've come to realize in this that, as somebody who is new in my place of ministry, it's really difficult for me to speak, as a white person, to white people about the racism of our city—what black voices in our city were very legitimately telling us which we should have attended to.

And to say it to a congregation that had been built on the history of fighting for race rights, fighting for inclusion, legally and otherwise with people, it was a really confusing, challenging thing. It was a huge valuable thing, but challenging. Our leaders would say, "We don't always agree with the way some protests went, but we understand that you have to be there. We understand that it's your call and that you have to discern where God is asking you to be and you have to discern that ethically and that you have a responsibility to us to call us forward as well even when we have a hard time." I also had people who got very involved right away, were present at protests. They were a few, but they were there. There are some lawyers who'd gotten very invested with Arch City Defenders and are doing a lot of work through them. We found that the conversation from the pulpit was hard on some people because they would feel unheard or felt sort of pushed beyond what was comfortable for them. So I started moving the conversation out of the sanctuary. It's still there in prayers. I still preach about it, but the whole sermon isn't just about this anymore. I found a way to nuance it, to invite people into further conversation, and now what we do is, after worship, we've had speakers. We've had conversations. We've had opportunities where people could be in dialogue and not just me preaching and some people agreeing and some people struggling and some people struggling because they agreed but they didn't want others to hurt.

Fuel for Something New

Mike Kinman is dean of Christ Church Cathedral, The Episcopal Cathedral of St. Louis. The church building is a National Historic Landmark located in downtown St. Louis.

On August 9, sometime in the afternoon, I remember checking Facebook, and Traci Blackmon had posted on her Facebook status something like this, "Sometimes something happens that makes you tear up your sermon and start over." And I thought, "Okay, what's going down?" Whenever I think something's going down, the first place I go is Twitter because that's usually where the best, fastest news comes. And I went to Twitter, and that's where I learned that this this young man had been – I think, at this point, I don't even think they knew his name – had been shot and killed.

We had just had Ruby Sales at Christ Church in February, and Ruby had educated us on extrajudicial killings by police of young African American men, so we knew a little bit about this. And I have to admit, and actually I'm a little ashamed to admit, my first reaction was "OK, so this happened again," and I didn't think much more of it.

And then about six the next morning, I got a message from Traci to call her. And she said, "I need you to be at the Ferguson Police

Department at three this afternoon. Would you be there to help do a prayer vigil?" And I said, "yes, absolutely," and then I went back and was looking on Facebook and Twitter... and I realized, oh, this is something. And I'm so grateful to Ruby Sales and to Susan Smith and to the people who had happened to be here [in February], and I mean nothing happens by accident. I really believe that we were prepared for this moment as Christ Church Cathedral.

The other thing for me is that August 9 was my last day of five weeks of vacation. And so I literally was coming off vacation. And talking with Traci, I realized she was right. This was one of those moments where you have to tear up your sermon. So I tore up my sermon. I knew I had to preach something different. I felt a call to name what was going on and what I saw beginning to happen even if I didn't know where it was headed.

The reading was one of my favorite scriptures, which is Peter being called out of the boat to walk on the water... and I realized this was a moment where we were being called to get out of the boat. We forget he actually walked on water and no one had ever done that before. He did something incredible. The disciples saw someone coming to them on the water, and Peter's test to see if it was Jesus was to ask him, "if it is you, bid me come out to you on the water." That's the way we know it's Jesus. Jesus tells us to do something impossible. If it isn't someone challenging us to do something that we think is impossible, it's probably not Jesus.... If the person said, "No. Stay in the boat and be comfortable," Peter would have known, "Oh, that's not Jesus. I don't know what that is, but that's not Jesus."

And so what I preached that morning was that we were born to walk on water, that we can do impossible things. That we were born to walk on water and it was time to step out of the boat. And as the first way of doing that, I invited everyone to join me at the Ferguson Police Department. I wanted to give people something that they could do. And the first thing that we always do is we pray. So it was interesting. I had all these plans for what the fall was going to be like and coming off vacation and I was going to get control of my calendar, and all of the sudden, it's just like God had other plans.

On Thursday morning, there was a Clergy Coalition meeting at Christ the King, and Derrick Robinson came in, and I had never met him before. He was really clear, and he basically said to this group of clergy sitting in these places of honor at high tables, "You need to get out in the streets with the young people. You need to not tell them to get into your churches, because they haven't been there and they're not going. You need to not go there in your suits and your collars and preach to them, because they don't care and they shouldn't care because we haven't been out there with them. You need to go out there and let them lead, and you need to listen." And I remember him saying, "You don't need to wear your suits. You need to wear your blue jeans." And I thought, "Yes. That's what we need to do." And that's what I have tried to do ever since....That was like this sort of the old church way of trying to do this, which, frankly, is so self-important and has no resonance at all nor should it. I mean, it is to the credit of the younger generation that they ain't buying it. Because it ain't worth buying. That was a turning point for me.

So from that point on, I have tried to keep asking myself, "Is this really about being with the young people? Is this about resourcing and fueling the new way the spirit is moving or is this about trying to hold onto old models?" I think old models have a role, but they're really fuel for something new. Frankly, if I'm going to look for a scriptural image for this, it's the despoiling of the Egyptians. It's when the people of Israel left slavery on Passover. They didn't go empty-handed. They were told to take the spoils from the Egyptians out with them. Grab what you can before you leave. Take the resources of the empire. It's incredibly subversive. In a beautifully subversive way, we can take the resources of the system and funnel them to resource a movement to transform the system. Especially as a Cathedral Dean, a big part of where I feel called is asking how can we work with that?

There's a great line in the musical *1776* where Stephen Hopkins, the representative from Rhode Island says, "In all my years I ain't never heard, seen, nor smelled an issue that was so dangerous it couldn't be talked about." That's one of my favorite quotes.

What drives me crazy is the stuff we're not talking about, the elephants in the room. If there's a truth, let's name it. It's about what we do in the Eucharist ... we lay our whole lives on the table with Christ. We don't hold anything back. And when we do that, God takes all of it—all of me, all of you, all of all of us and all of Jesus—and turns it into resurrection life that gets sent out into the world.

So whenever there's a significant issue in the congregation, we just have what we call an "On the Table Forum." We use this Eucharistic model and say this is not about problem solving or micromanaging. It is about laying our lives and our thoughts and our feelings on the table. It's so that any issue at all can be laid on the table and we'll talk about it. And we very well may not resolve it, but we'll talk about it.

By Tuesday night, I knew we needed to have one of these and just give people a place to process. So after that first week of the protests and the tear gas and the rubber bullets and of our city becoming the identified patient for American racism on national TV, on that next Sunday (August 17), we had one of these forums after church. It was a holy moment. We were there for about an hour and then gathered at the foot of the cross and we prayed together and we sang. I'm always amazed at how vulnerable people will allow themselves to be in those forums. It truly is holy, but broadly speaking, what came out of that was white people saying, "I can't believe this is happening in my city." And it was people of color saying, "I can't believe it took this long for this to happen in our city." And that was a huge epiphany for me.

From the beginning, our response to this, as a region, has mirrored our fragmentation. And one of the things I was convicted of immediately is how much a part of the problem I am. And a piece of that is me asking myself, "So how many people do I know who live north of Delmar? How many relationships do I have? How much time do I spend north of Delmar?" I pride myself on being really progressive. I've done all this antiracism training. I'm downtown with people struggling with homelessness. I'm all this. I'm all that. If I had thought on sort of a learning curve with racism, it's like "I've got to be up here." But what I've realized is I'm not up high. I'm down low. And maybe I've moved a few degrees upward on that curve since August 9, and that few degrees has rocked my world. The biggest thing I'm conscious of is how much more I have to learn.

Hitting Home

Shaun Jones is the assistant pastor of Mt. Zion Baptist Church Complex in St. Louis, where his father is the senior pastor. Shaun is also the secretary of the Clergy Coalition in St. Louis. He describes the impact of the Ferguson events "hitting home," as well as his calling to bridge the gap between the older pastors and young protestors.

I was born in Cool Valley, which is right outside of Ferguson. So West Florissant and Florissant Road are familiar places for me. I attended elementary school in Ferguson Florissant School District. My mother, who is a retired educator, taught at Ferg Florissant her entire career.

As a result, Ferguson has always been very near and dear to me. Even as we protested, I protested right on the street where I get my eyeglasses from as a kid [laughs]. So to see this happen in my home is very disheartening. I've always been socially conscious. I was upset when I learned about the injustices and killing of black men in New York, Florida, and other parts of the U.S. However, you think, "That's there." But, when it hits home, it's—it's something a little bit more painful, a little bit more knee-jerking that these are streets I grew up on. These are places I go. These are neighborhoods I have members who live in, and then, all of the sudden, this has just really hit the home front.

As I've traveled across the country recently for the Clergy Coalition, I want people to understand that Ferguson is a suburb. I think, sometimes, people get certain, quote unquote, ideas that young, black men who have confrontations with police officers must be from bad neighborhoods, must be in drug-infested neighborhoods. But when you see Canfield Apartments, Canfield Greens, you see homes. You see a grassy area where children are playing and hanging out. You see grandmothers going back and forth. You see people going to work, living their regular, everyday lives. Yet when you see the street where it happened still stained with blood and you see this memorial, which is now surrounded by teddy bears, posters, and balloons that have now deflated and are on the ground, it gives you a powerful image that literally he was killed in the street, literally on his grandmother's street.

I truly believe when anyone visits the site something has to resonate with them. Anybody who has any concept of human life, who believes in the sanctity of life has to be moved by some compassion regardless of what you believe Officer Darren Wilson or Michael Brown should or should not have done.. The community continues to say this is not a place that we can forget about.

I as an officer in the Clergy Coalition, I feel that part of my calling is an attempt to bring the old guard into the 21st century ministry and particularly to understand the hurts, the cries, the frustrations, the issues that this generation has to deal with everyday. This has fueled my work within the Clergy Coalition because many didn't understand why people, particularly young people, responded in Ferguson the way they did. Many did not get it. St Louis only really had like one major protest, which was the Jefferson Bank protest back in 1963.[1]

And in talking to a colleague friend of mine, he really helped me to see that many of the older black clergy we have now, they witnessed the press conference side of the 1960s Civil Rights Movement, but missed out on the grassroots, streets organizing part of the movement.

Thus some of these leaders struggle to understand those in the streets and the community struggles to understand these leaders. The only vantage point they have of these leaders are either what they see on the news, what they hear from black comedians joking about black preachers as being pimps in the pulpit or players or taking money from members, and they don't see the good works that many of the African American clergy have done over the past decades.

_____

[1]A recent article about the Jefferson Bank protest can be found at http://www. stltoday.com/news/local/metro/look-back/look-back-civil-rights-efforts-in-st-louis-build-toward/article_5fb6c94d-4d7b-5069-b5c1-37cb9283dccd.html.

Jesus, before he ever preached the Kingdom of God is at hand, before he attempted to bring people into the understanding that he was to fulfill the law, he spent time with people. He met their needs. He healed them. He fed them. He spent time with what other folk called sinners—went to their homes, broke bread with them. They got to know him. He got to know them. And the times, the nights we would spend out at night there and be engaged with the daytime—even the day that we spent hours outside of the St. Ann Police Department almost all day to get them out of jail one night—created that nexus of community and relationship where we began —we became one versus separate entities.

The ministry of presence, I think, is something that the church needs to understand. They may not come to you, but if you go to them, not on your high horse saying, "I offer you this," but just say, "I'm here for you. I want to get to know you. What can you offer us?" We, the clergy who met people in the street repented when we met and spent time with our young people. We apologized for not getting it. We apologized for the inconsistent presence of the black church in the community before this moment. We approached them with humility, not with position, not with title. We came with the idea that we're not better than you, but we want to learn from you. Your passion, your commitment, your sacrifice has inspired us.

We continued to make this statement over and over again, as we conversed with young people in the movement, so that they understood and we understood. So the fact that they kept seeing us out there night after night with them, not trying to tell them what to do but saying, "We've got your back. What can we do to help? We have this idea. What do you think about it?" Because, oftentimes, a church wants to tell people what to do versus saying, "If we're all part of the church together, then what does the church want to do? What does the community want to do and what role do you see yourself playing in this movement?"

By no means have we, as a church, tried to own this movement. We've tried to say that we can be a part of this movement, and we have a part to play. They have a part, but we can work together with them, and so I think the idea of working together and connecting with one another is when I believe churches in St. Louis became active participants in the movment.

The next chapter turns our attention to the emergence of leadership among young adults, and their experiences of the role of clergy in the movement.

Mary Gene Boteler (first on left), Heather Arcovitch (fourth from left), Deb Krause (fifth), and Rebecca Ragland (sixth) join with clergy and others to pray in downtown St. Louis. *(Photo by Betsy Reznicek)*

Shaun Jones at protest in Clayton, seat of St. Louis County government. *(AP photo)*

CHAPTER 4

Jesus Is in the Streets!

"Strength, courage, and wisdom... And it's been inside of me all along."

India.Arie

One of the undeniable truths that came out of the Ferguson-related events was the strength, power, and presence of young people. Not only their physical strength, but also the emotional fortitude they exerted to carry on the quest for racial justice hundreds of days after Michael Brown was killed. Millennials, the moniker given to people born between 1980 and the middle of the first decade of the 2000s, took to the streets *en masse* in the days, weeks, and months following Michael Brown's death. They strategized, organized, and rallied to demand justice on behalf of Michael Brown, and their voices resonated with the quest for racial justice around the world.

One of the most poignant ways their collective voice was heard was during a Ferguson October event titled "Mass Meeting on Ferguson," an Interfaith Service on October 12. More than a thousand people attended this event at the Chaifetz Arena on the Saint Louis University campus. The purpose of the gathering was to mix faith and activism by having prayers and speeches offered by clergy and community leaders, and Dr. Cornel West was scheduled to headline the evening with a closing speech and call to action. The event started with a parade of clergy from various faith traditions and community leaders making their presentations. However, after about an hour or so of speeches, I could hear rumblings emerge from many young people in the audience. Then out of the rumblings came a loud, booming voice that said, "This is some bull****!" The young people, many of who had been protesting in Ferguson, every day, for more than 60 days, had had enough of the talking from people with whom they did not seem to connect. Once this declaration was made, more young people stood up and started saying, "Let them speak!"

This was a powerful experience for me, because it provided an opportunity for the audience to hear from the young activists in their words, and on their terms. It was a powerful experience of awakening to witness—a palpable shift in the energy in the arena that went from a "same old, same old" feeling to a charged energy when the young people spoke up. It was organized chaos at its best. They were not tolerating business as usual, which has been endemic of the movement. Disrupting the *status quo* has been at the core of the protests. They were determined to not just sit quietly and wait their turn because the urgency of the situation demanded immediate attention and responsiveness, and they embodied that urgency that night.

After the "let them speak" demands gained momentum and volume, young activists emerged from the audience and started walking toward the stage. The crowd cheered. The dozens of media reps, most of who had been hanging back from the stage, woke up and swooped to the edge of the stage. The moderator, Traci Blackmon, stood at the podium and said, "The next voice we will hear will be a word from the streets." The crowd stood to their feet and cheered wildly and some like me shed a few tears of joy and pride.

The young activists spoke passionately, among other things, about the reasons they became involved in this movement for racial justice. Tef Poe, a recording artist from St. Louis, told the crowd that they're just regular people trying to solve a difficult problem. He said "We're not trained organizers. We're not professional activists. We're just real people who identify the problem and decided to go do something about it." He also called for clergy to get up and join them, which was a recurring theme for many of the clergy already involved.

The quest for black people to be seen as *fully* human is a significant component of this movement for racial justice. Many young activists resonated with this idea. They related to Mike Brown's *humanity,* and felt that those who were sworn to serve and protect Brown disrespected him. To them, Mike Brown was not a thug or "Hulk Hogan," as Officer Darren Wilson described him in his grand jury testimony. He was a human being who deserved to be treated as such. So it was not surprising that so many young black people responded because they too resonated with this kind of dehumanization.

All of the young activists I interviewed went to Ferguson as soon as they were able. Jamell Spann, a young activist who lives in St. Louis, was visiting a friend near the Ferguson Police Department the day Brown was killed, and protested daily for months afterward.

> And a friend of mine who lived in Canfield witnessed the incident and was live-tweeting it. I was watching everything he had to say about it on his Twitter account as it happened. And I was like, "Wow," and I texted him. I started talking about it more, and the friend whose house I was visiting, they live fairly close to the Ferguson Police Department. So as I was leaving their house, I saw a large group of people gathering in front of the police department demanding that the police answer for what they did or release a statement or come and talk to them. And I stood with them as soon as I saw them. I can't really explain what drove me to the police station or outside, but when something like this happens, close to where you lay your head, your city, your backyard, it kind of has this magnetizing effect on you that you don't really pay attention to the "why" when it's going on. You just know what and how you feel about what needs to be done.

Brittany Ferrell and Alexis Templeton, co-founders of Millennial Activists United (MAU), were both out of town when Brown was killed. They stayed connected to the unfolding events via Twitter while they were away, and became a visible presence in Ferguson once they returned. Templeton said:

> I got off the plane on the 15 of August, and I hit the ground, and I've been there ever since. I saw what happened [while I was away]... I was glued to my phone. Once I started to see people getting tear-gassed and things like that... It was crazy. So when it was time to go home, I got on the plane, and as soon as I got off the plane, I got to my car, and I went down on the ground, and I've been there ever since.

Ferrell, the mother of a young child, also saw that the scene in Ferguson had progressively worsened since the day Brown was killed, and responded promptly.

> I got home at 11:00 p.m. Wednesday night the 13th. I checked my Twitter to see what was going on, and it was the same old thing that I had seen for the past couple of days: police tear-gassing citizens, shooting them with rubber bullets, basically treating them as less than human. And I decided that I was going to wait until the morning to hit the ground, and that's exactly what I did. I went home. I unpacked. I was on Twitter all night long. I don't know when I fell asleep, but as soon as I woke up the next day,…the first thing I did, I picked up my daughter, and we went to Ferguson."

All of the Millennial activists I interviewed learned about Michael Brown's death through social media. One of the touch points about Millennial activism in Ferguson was its primary dependency upon social media for gathering and spreading information. They were often suspicious of the network news reports, and preferred to gather their information from people whose statements did not have to go through corporate-interest-sponsored media filters. Tef Poe wielded credibility among the people on the ground during his speech at the Chaifetz Arena when he said

> All the stuff that y'all saw on CNN, we ain't need CNN for that because we got off our ass and went there and talked to Pookie and Ray Ray that live in Canfield and found out what happened. I didn't need MSNBC. Darnell told me. Darnell told me he died with his hands up. So I believe Darnell. I don't need Don Lemon to confirm what happened because I'm there.

Being present was the hallmark of their engagement in this movement. Their bodies and their physical presence are what gave credence to their efforts. This is what makes one's absence so palpable because this was not an ideological movement, but a process in which bodies were taking to the streets to be seen and heard in the quest for justice.

Few were surprised by the outcry over Michael Brown's death as they named the racial tension that they perceived to exist in St. Louis. Brittany Ferrell describes it this way:

It wasn't until like a day or two [after Aug. 9], when I began seeing the police face to face with civilians, police in riot gear, civilians just unarmed in regular, plain clothes. And they just had juxtaposed that photo next to the one from the '60s, and I was like, "Wow, that's very similar to what it looked like back in the '60s." And then I began to see photos of K-9 units and video recorders, video recordings of police officers calling protestors "animals" and telling them that they'll "blow their f-ing brains out." And that's when I was like this is violence from the people that are supposed to protect the community. And I've always known that racism was brewing in this city. I've always seen it. I've always experienced it even though it was subtle. I've always been very sensitive to the racial bias that people in this city, in particular, had. It was very covert and—or so they thought.

Jamell Spann describes it this way:

I think it's been a powder keg long before Mike Brown was murdered. Back in the early to mid '90s, when I was like really little, like only two or three years old, there was—there's a lot of history in this city about racial tension with the police, a long history of—especially towards the eastern side of St. Louis and in East St. Louis itself, there's been a lot of racial tension with the police, a lot of going back and forth over the years. And the fact that that became so common after a while is because people got desensitized to what was happening, especially in the downtown neighborhoods. And me growing up downtown, you always felt like, yeah, people—the murder rate is high in this city in general, and the fact that people get used to it kind of speaks for kind of sometimes how desensitized people get to it. But I honestly think it was because so much of it was like what's happened in the city for so long, especially in regards to the police, I think. It wasn't that there was something special or unique about it. It was the fact that you're finally seeing the voice of a city that's just been fed up.

I come from a family that really places a lot of focus on the beauty and the strength behind being black and being conscious and not taking everything for face value. More so than being told what to think, I was challenged to think and to think differently, and when you're told to think you generally only think about what appeases the people who are telling you to think. But when you're challenged to think and left to draw any conclusions of your own, you sort of end up with a questioning nature. You don't just sit back and accept what anybody hands you. And I think that just kind of grew with me into an adult, especially when it comes in terms of observing police behavior because, coming from a military family, you hold people who wear a badge, who are trusted to have a weapon in sort of a different and higher light than you would of a normal person because you're taught to appreciate the weight of responsibility and you question that responsibility when it's not being directed in an appropriate way.

Brittany Ferrell also grew up with a lot of questions about the injustices she witnessed, and previous activism was a precursor to her Ferguson involvement.

I've done activism. It was just different. Before August 9, most of my activist work was on food justice and food equality. When they shut down the Schnucks [grocery store] on North Grand, that was a huge issue. And I started having conversations with OBS [Organization for Black Struggle], a few other community organizers around—conversations around doing like an inner city co-op and what that might look like to bring fresh food and fresh produce to our food desert in the city. [Growing up] I just always had a lot of unanswered questions. I had a lot of questions. No one had the answers. When you would like to seek solutions, no one had any. So I remember I would spend a lot of my time thinking about the "what ifs" or coming up with ideas. And then, after like—after so many years of studying and so many years of networking with the right people, I was able to launch my first program that was rooted in health and nutrition, and it had amazing reviews. So it was activism but it was just a different kind of activism. When I saw what happened, after

August 9, I knew that it was only a matter of time before it just blew up and became what it is now.

Perceived Role of the Church

I was very curious to know how the young activists perceived the role of the church, and what their engagement with clergy had been thus far. All of the young activists I interviewed had particular thoughts about the nature of the church and what "church folks" should be doing at such a time as this. While there was no sense that the "church" at large had done anything heroic related to Ferguson, they did have several interactions with clergypeople that were markedly different from pervious experiences of "church." Alexis Templeton juxtaposes two visits to two different congregations and raises critical questions about the nature and purpose of the church.

What makes it hard to find anything redemptive about the Christian faith is… obviously, the contradictions in the Bible, but also the people who read the Bible are very contradicting when it comes to their faith, when it comes to this book. They're very—they take certain parts out. They pick it apart, and they throw at you what they want you to hear. But they don't expect you, as a nonbeliever, somebody who doesn't even go to church every Sunday, to be able to throw back what they missed. So "You might have read John 13:12, but John 13:12 through 16 says this…" [laughs] So no, it's very hard to find anything redemptive about church. But in this fight, we went to Starsky's [Wilson] church, and that was the first time I'd been to church in a while. He talked about how Jesus himself was a revolutionary. I'm like, well, here we go. Thank God. Somebody finally said something worth listening to, and not because that's what I wanted to hear but because that's not taught.

[Recently] I went to church when my grandparents had Bible study. I popped in, and the pastor was saying that the people in Ferguson needed to come to the church, but the punchline of his church is… "Go out into the world and do." So I'm like, "The line of your church is, 'Go out into the world and do,' but the people of Ferguson are supposed to step away from the world to come into your church to get the word of God, to take it back out to the people. That doesn't make sense." But Starsky [Wilson] was saying the church is in Ferguson. Every night, around 9:00, when they start bringing the riot gear out, that's where church is. It came from when he was talking about how Jesus went into the tabernacle and he turned over the tables...because of the corruption and the B.S. that was going on, and Jesus was like, "Nah." And he's like, "That's what's happening in Ferguson. It's a bunch of "Jesuses" standing at the tabernacle, which happens to be the Ferguson Police Department, and they're flipping over the tables. And I'm like, "That's real. That's exactly what's happening right now." The corruption in that part of the story, when it came to Jesus, was money, I believe. But, in this instance, it's ticketing, which leads to the warrants, which leads to you putting money in your pockets. You're pulling people over to make sure they get a ticket, so they have to pay you money because that keeps your light bill on at your station. You're killing people. God knows how much that pays because now you have to pay overtime to keep these police out here in riot gear. So you relate it back to that story perfectly. So when he said that, I'm like, "Yo, that's the realest thing I've heard from a preacher in years because it's the actual truth." That's literally in the book.

Clearly, Alexis was exposed to a different way of framing the works of Jesus that resonated with her, and her personal experience with clergy on the ground in Ferguson made room for her to see them in a different light. She goes on to say:

And he [Starsky Wilson] showed scripture, and I love that. So yes, I guess you could call that a redemptive moment because this movement has also showed me that there are clergy members like Traci Blackmon, Rabbi Susan, and Starsky who know what they're talking about and who are in it for the right reason and are not only just reaping the benefits—because there's definitely benefits to being a minister or a rabbi or what have you. But, actually following the steps of the shepherd...while being a shepherd—which means all your sheep are following you (which is dope)—that's exactly where the faith is. So even though Rabbi

Susan [Talve] is of Jewish faith, it's the same thing. Like she still sees it as the same thing. God was a revolutionary. He did this, this, and this. He started this. That's a revolutionary act, but she still gets out there, and she stands with people who don't even look like her because that's what God did. That's what Jesus— that's—well, she don't believe in Jesus, but that's what God did. He stood up for the people that didn't look like him that were made in his image but did not exactly look like him. And she believes if everybody's made in God's image, then everybody out there is a part of God. So she needs to be out there too. So people like that and then like Mike Kinman, they make you believe that there is God even if not everybody's God is the same God. But those four's God right there got to be the same God because they get it.

Brittany Ferrell also witnessed a different type of church model through the clergy involvement in Ferguson, and how they became part of the church that came to them.

I think the clergy involvement has showed me that the church does not always have to exist within those four walls. I feel like there's this perpetuated idea that "church" is something you go to, and it's been proven wrong within the last six months, because church has come to us whether we welcomed it or not. It was there. We became church. People who have not ever prayed or who have not prayed in years prayed that night on that lot of that police department. [laughs]

That's real. Church came to us whether we realized it or not. I feel like church is omnipresent, like it's everywhere. You create church wherever you go if you embody that God likeness. It's not something that you drive to and you park and you get out and you sit in there for two hours.

The clergy who engaged with young protestors demonstrated a very particular kind of embodiment of scripture and faith. According to Alexis Templeton, they were not biblical literalists, but rather sought meaning through scripture in connection with their work for justice.

They often embodied a prayerful presence that was perceived to have an impact on the situations and reflected the kind of love that Jesus talked about in scripture.

> The Bible does not just say love they neighbor. It tells you what love is, so that you know exactly how to identify it and what love definition you need to live by when you have to get up out your pews and get out in those streets and love on these various, different black people, these various different people no matter what shape or size they may come in. So it has shown that the church is stubborn, that some churches are very stubborn, but it also has shown that some black churches are the black sheep, ironically. And they come out, and they do exactly what the Bible says without doing exactly what the Bible says. They're fluid in their spirituality, and they're fluid in their reading of this book. And, actually, the more fluid you are with it,...the better your understanding is of it. When you're fluid in the Word, you live better because you're not constantly looking for the literal meaning in these scriptures. You're moving. You're just letting the word push you. You're letting it come out of you. That's what you're supposed to do. And that's what Starskys [Wilson] and Traci Blackmons and your [Osagyefo] Sekous, that's what they have done. That's what the Mike Kinmans—that's what they've gotten up and done, and this has taught me that this is what the church is supposed to be. They have taught me to believe in God, and that's real. It was all in their walk. It was all in their ability to step back for a minute and be a sheep of the people. They allowed the Godlike features of the people to show them, in a better sense, what God is and what God is about and what God did with what God wants. They took a step back. They didn't have to say anything. Starsky comes out in the little Brooks Brothers hat and his sweatpants and stuff and like there's nothing preacher-like about him. He's just a regular black dude...but it's all in that walk. It's all in his ability to not say anything sometimes, to just be there, to be present and to bow his head. And that's when Godlike things come out, when he knows something's about to go down and he just has to be a part of it because he's standing with his people, and he just puts his head down, and he says a prayer.

There have been times they have prayed and—the police didn't come. And I don't think people notice that, and that will make you believe in God yourself because we just got arrested last night. [laughs] But because you decide to get down and not even get down—sometimes, they'll just stand there. You look over and just know that they're praying. And you'll be like, "Man, the police—where'd the police go?" [laughs] It's real. That is no exaggeration at all.

Jamell Spann describes the clergy presence in this way:

I first began paying attention to clergy once I had noticed that they were around, but that they were being quiet. During the early stages, the clergy were out, and they'd march with us or they'd be present to do a prayer for a vigil. But there were a few, whether they were clergy or whether they were just the members of any faith or church, they'd be out to lead a chant or to try to lead a march. But it was afterwards I kind of paid attention to the clergy's obvious stance of position that they would sort of hang back. That's when they caught my attention because I knew they were doing it for a reason. I just didn't know why yet. And, a while after that, when we'd be having one of our usual "Mexican standoffs" with the police—they'd be in their riot gear with their guns and their tear gas standing in front of the police station or on the street, and the rest of us would have shirts that say, "Unarmed civilian," or signs, our words face-to-face with them—the clergy would come out during really stressful moments that looked as if they could go either way, and they would say a brief prayer, and they would stand with us. They didn't try to take over or commandeer our protest. They gave us the space and the ability we needed, as young people, to shift the narrative in the direction we felt it should go. They didn't try to hijack it from us, and I think the whole thing about there being an age divide or stuff like that are kind of excuses that people use to, like, automatically rule out any, I guess, bipartisanship between young and old people or people with different views on the movement. But I thought what they were doing was noble when I saw a couple of things like that. They show up, and they lend us their bodies and their strength and their prayer, and they let us take actions and push things in the way that we felt it should go. To me, it showed a shift in consciousness, a favorable shift in consciousness. I like to view myself as sort of like a nonchalant, pretty Buddhist type of person. I don't have one particular hard stance on religion. I'm really open-minded and generally accepting.

Protestors Arrested and Taken to St. Ann Police Station

Another example of the way the clergy lent their bodies and strength and prayer was when 13 young protestors were arrested in front of the Ferguson police station on October 3. In this instance, the clergy played an active role in assisting the young protestors. Starsky Wilson, pastor of St. John's UCC and CEO of the Deaconess Foundation, reflects on how he understood the presence of clergy in this situation.

I got an e-mail inviting clergy to go down to the St. Ann Police Department because 13 protestors had been arrested on the street the night before for a noise ordinance violation that either of us would get a $150.00 fine sent to our house. And so on this Friday, a group of clergy gathered and we ended up spending all day negotiating with the police chief, rotating visitation to these young people. Only two at a time could go back initially, so we asked if all of the young people could come out. We were also working on trying to get a judge on the phone, trying to get lawyers working on this. We had the unfortunate circumstance of being there on a day when there was the investiture of a federal judge, so all the legal community that we could potentially get were all in this ceremony. So it was tough getting the folks together. But I say this to say that on that day, we spent spiritual capital, social capital, and privilege. Ultimately, a pastor was very helpful in connecting with the judge that we needed to get these young people, largely (everybody except for two), released on their own recognizance.

And we got to be, that day, present with those young people. We got to minister to them spiritually. We got to meet their physical needs, including basic stuff like, "Hey, Police Chief, if Brittany could release her personal effects to me then we can go pick up her car, so it doesn't get towed." And to use our social capital for the sake of their protection and care—and, that day, I think we began to—and people were—some folks that were already doing this, but I think we began to, as a unit and as a network, commit to doing that more systematically. And I think that was an appropriate role going forward, so that we could, on the line at night, stand beside them, stand with them, sometimes stand behind them, pray for them but be present with them and build ongoing relationship such that we can provide ministries of presence, if not care, when they are desired. Affirming that what they're doing is, in many ways, "church." Even if they wouldn't call it that, it is the mission of the church. And saying that to them because you'll find, so many times, Alexis [Templeton] quotes scripture up and down, goes to church just to make her grandma happy. and people on Twitter calling her everything but a child of God. So she quotes scripture back to them and she is not looking it up. It's in her.

So in many ways, it's necessary, redemptive to be able to say that because it's just not what they know. Shame on us, but this is not what they've known. So I think those have been our roles and responsibilities: to affirm, to be present, to provide care as asked, and to protect though all that. I don't mean that in a paternalistic way, but our presence protects them because police act differently when we're around. And I think a lot of that was crystallized for at least me on that day.

Mike Kinman, dean of the Christ Church Cathedral, describes his own awakening as he sought to help the young protestors get out of jail. He describes this experience in relation to the Civil Rights Movement, and why it was so profound for him. He begins his reflection at the point when the St. Ann police allowed the clergy to sit in the same room together with the young protestors while they were still in police custody.

"We're going to let you all come in a room together." So they cleared out the city council/courtroom. And they brought these young people and most of them are women, and it was Brittany and Ashley and Alexis and this sort of group and then, those of us who were clergy, who were there, probably about the same number. And they're all there in their orange jumpsuits, and we're all there. We're all sitting in this circle together, and, of course, as soon as they come in, the first thing they ask is, "Can we have your phones?"

And we gave them to them, and they're texting and tweeting and doing all this stuff, and they're activating their networks. And I'm just sitting back and watching them, and I'm watching them relate to each other. And I'm watching them talk, and I'm watching their joy and their humor, but also, it's not immaturity. There's a strength.

I was born in 1968, so I wasn't alive for the Civil Rights Movement. But I've done a lot of reading, and the names—Diane Nash and Jim Lawson and Bernard Lafayette and John Lewis and Marion Barry—are icons to me. One of my life goals is I really want to meet Diane Nash at some point. She is just one of my heroes.

And I was sitting there watching these young people and particularly watching the young women, and I had this—for me, it was an epiphany. And it was that these names, like I'm reading John Lewis's memoir right now and it's incredible, and John Lewis is just this giant and this icon and this amazing person. But John Lewis didn't start off that way. No one does. He was a kid at one point.

And I thought, "You know what? 1958, 1959, '60, '61, at Fisk University and at these different places—oh, my God, I bet that's what Diana Nash looked like. I bet that's what Jim Lawson looked like. And what I realized in that moment was I was just in awe, and I get to be here, and I have choices to make. When this story is told, will I have helped them or not? Will I have tried to make this about me or not? And I thought, 20 and 30 years from now, we are going to know the names of Alexis Templeton and Brittany Ferrell and DeRay McKesson and Netta Elzie, and we're going to know these names. And we're going to be so proud they were from here, and we're going to pretend we weren't spitting on them at the time. And we're going to deny that we did.

And, I said, "My God, thank you, Lord Jesus, for letting me be in this room." And I knew then that it's like: "'No, this is what I have to be about because I refuse to, when this history of this moment is written, I refuse to have Christ Church Cathedral play anything less than the role that pointed to the young people." And that's why, since then, I just keep saying, "What can we do to help them?"

That moment at the St. Ann Police Department, that was the most profound moment of this entire experience for me... because it was the first time I realized, "Oh, my, oh, my God. This is who this is! This is what Diane Nash looks like. This is what James Lawson looks like. This is what Bernard Lafayette looks like and thank you, God, for letting me be here and for giving me the opportunity to choose...," and it's an ongoing choice every day.

Jamell Spann was one of the first protestors arrested that evening. He describes the role of the clergy and the mutuality engendered in this moment:

When I saw the clergy sort of make their stance, I already had high expectations for them. Once I saw that they were willing to get locked up not just with us but also in our stead, once me and twelve other people were wrongly arrested one night—I'll always stand that we were wrongly arrested because we were protesting standing on the sidewalk. We got transferred to St. Ann. The night they took all of us there, we were on the Ferguson Police Department lot, and I was the first one they arrested and then everybody else showed up and got arrested because I got arrested. And the next day, the clergy took it upon themselves to negotiate the terms of our release, and it took a lot of work on their part, and that's when we—I, personally, and a lot of us started developing personal bonds with the clergy because that was—like, that was a beautiful thing. It really showed that there were—they were trying to initiate the passing of the torch and the shift in consciousness, so people could get more involved, yet accepting of the fact that our position is just here to support. And a lot of people don't really know what support is or looks like, but the clergy demonstrated that by giving us the strength to do what we felt was right. They didn't come with any terms or conditions. They didn't try to impose what they thought on any of us. It was sort of like a blind trust you can get energy from. And after they showed up in St. Ann when they put us in those disgusting orange jumpsuits and they let us exit ourselves and all sit as a unit while we talked to the clergy who were sitting as a unit, we learned that, okay, working with them isn't—having them around pays off... This isn't so bad. [laughs] The fact that they stepped back and let us do what we felt we should do, and we, in turn, gave them the space to support us or work out what they felt they needed to do without us trying to run them, it was—they respected us enough to give us the space to do whatever we felt we had to do, and we, in turn, respected them for giving us their trust. So it was like a mutual respect between the clergy and us at that point. We saw how dedicated and committed they were, like it was kind of a beautiful thing to sit back and let somebody show you how much they support you.

Every time one of them gets arrested, we're right at the jail with them waiting on them to get out the same way they did for us. We made sure to reciprocate all of the love and respect we felt that we got from them. I know I do.

Reciprocity, not Respectability

One of the pet peeves that constantly emerged was the idea of respectability politics. The young protestors regularly renounced respectability politics because, in their view, it has been of no import for the well-being of black people in America. In other words, no matter how well dressed, well educated and well spoken a black person was, he or she was still not accepted by white people in America. The racialized critiques of President and Mrs. Obama, two Ivy-League–educated lawyers who have been heard regularly across cable news and radio for the past eight years, often serve as evidence that black people can never be fully accepted in white America. So in this movement for racial justice, young people are not bound by the illusion of acceptance if they just are "respectable" enough, and they are talking and acting in ways that are authentic to how they truly feel.

Jamell Spann describes respectability politics in this way:

And respectable politics are a type of political viewpoint that seeks change, power, or recognition through appeasing...the system rather than opposing it on just about every level, like I feel it should be. And you can't gain your freedom or you can't gain more power by appealing to...to the humanity of a social construct that proves to you that it has none. You can't appeal to the better side of a person who has no better side, honestly.

Respectability politics is saying that, instead of marching in the streets, we should be pulling our pants up and wearing ties, and that we can solve all of our problems by voting even though, sometimes, elections just come down to the lesser of two evils; that, if we put all of our faith and energy and money into the same things we've been doing the for the past 60, 70 years, if we try to integrate with the system and fight back again, we'll be better off than trying to create our own or use our own voices or oppose it and disrupt it on every level.

And I think respectability comes with a lot of comfortability. A lot of people are comfortable in wearing suits and ties and putting their faith in ballots and trying to live up to what a lot of our oppressors and people say how we should act. A lot of being far too comfortable and complacent enough to not change lives within respectability politics, and whether people want to admit that or not, some shade of that I would say exists in every single black person who doesn't really support this movement. Some shade of them wanting to appear like fine, decent, upstanding young black folks because, you know, that's what America says. Like this is the only type of black person we're going to respect or acknowledge: the one who wears the suit and tie and talks about voting and does this. I've yet to find a decent-like adjective to describe it other than silly.

Oftentimes, it's just tiring to see people—your own people, your own brothers and your sisters—saying stuff that they should know better. It hasn't gotten us anywhere yet. It takes different tactics and a different mindset for a different battle or a different war, and I just mean that figuratively. I mean, in many senses, the police in this system have waged, like, an emotional, spiritual, and physical war on black folks, and to see people who cannot recognize that or are so comfortable with doing or trying or putting absolute faith in things we've been doing for so long without coming out of their comfort zone and thinking or trying anything new is disheartening because it holds back a lot of progress that we could be making and that we could have made a long time ago.

Millennial Activists United came together because they fundamentally believed that all black lives matter, and wanted to create a space for that vision to have life and expression. Brittany Ferrell and Alexis Templeton reflect the intersectionality of the movement—that is, the convergence of their peers of different races, gender, class, and sexual orientation. Brittany begins by sharing how the group emerged.

After we went out to protest, we began to see the same faces, and we began to see the same faces in the same places regardless to whether we were in front of the police department, like, elbowing our way to the front because the people that were doing the work were not in front of the cameras. So it came a point when we all just kind of came together, and anything that we do, we did it together. And there was a certain—we had just a common theme: it was that we were all black and we were mostly women. We were fairly young, and we were a part of that LGBTQ community, the majority of us were. And being woman, being young, being LGBTQ and black, you're automatically marginalized. So when you're in this fight for justice with other black folks, being a woman and being LGBTQ and being young, you're marginalized within the black community. So there was this need to, like, create a space for people who were actively engaged in doing this work, who were committed to it, who were sacrificing and giving up everything to do this work—and not for them to do the work and then the people who are not doing the work being in front of the cameras. [It should be] for them to do the work and to be able to vocalize what is happening in the city that they're doing the work in.

So I had to create that space. So it was just a bunch of likeminded people coming together who were recognizing the similarities and then decided to create a body, like a "safe zone," in which people can exist who would often be marginalized, and that's how Millennial Activists United started.

Alexis Templeton

At first, people were like, "Okay." [laughs] But, now, it's turned into like the gay people were trying to take over the black movement and hijack the movement with their own agendas about gay rights. And I'm just like, "No." I just happen to be black and gay at the same time. So you get a lot more anger. You become more sensitive to things people say and things people do that "marginalize the marginalized," if you will. You start to get really sensitive to the sexist comments that people make and really sensitive—hypersensitive—to everything around you, the inner aspects of the movement instead of like focusing on the police. You also—you get sensitive to how there aren't any women police officers on the frontlines. There ain't black women police officers on the frontline... So you just start to pay attention, pay a lot more attention to what's going on, and your heart gets bigger because your fight gets bigger.

Brittany Ferrell

Right now, our organization is much smaller than it was when we started, but the core values are still pretty much the same. It's advocating for black life, and that's inclusionary of all black life. It's inclusive to not just heterosexual black men, but it's inclusive to black life that's gay, straight, bi, transgender, poor, well off, educated, uneducated—just black life because I feel like, without that important piece, we would oftentimes put black life on a hierarchy of this black life is worth fighting for, but this black life isn't really worth it, and this black life maybe if we have time because, right now, we're advocating for this black life. So we can't do that in this fight. It's divisive, and it's just not constructive. Being young, with this generational gap that exists in this movement, being young and black, not being—not upholding respectability politics but just being unapologetic and wanting to be accepted. Just wanting to just be respected for you existing as you are.

Alexis and I hosted some breakout sessions at the Ferguson Commission meeting one Saturday when they had it for the youth. One trend that was in my breakout session was [really] young people.[1] The age range was about 14 to 24. The trend was "wanting to be accepted." Most of the young people in all three of my sessions said, "I just really wish sometimes my parents would tell me that they believe that I can do whatever it is," or, "That they encourage me as I am and not make me feel like I have to be 'fixed' before I can achieve something." And that was just a small piece of the population of the young people that are involved in the actual movement. So I'm quite sure that those sentiments of wanting to be accepted as you are can be applied to most of the young people who are involved in this movement. They just want to be accepted. And we're still advocating for that.

---

[1]The Ferguson Commission website describes the commission as "an empowered, independent and diverse group that will study the underlying social and economic conditions underscored by the unrest in the wake of the death of Michael Brown. Openness and transparency will be cornerstones of the Commission's work." The commission was formed by Missouri Governor Jay Nixon under executive order. http://stlpositivechange.org/ accessed on January 20, 2015.

Crowd cheers as the young activists prepare to speak at an interfaith gathering at Chaifetz Arena on October 12. *(Photo by Christian Goodman*/St. Louis Post-Dispatch/ *Polaris)*

Activist and recording artist Tef Poe leaves the stage at the Chaifetz Arena. *(Photo by Christian Goodman*/St. Louis Post-Dispatch/*Polaris)*

Clergy arranging for protestors to be released from the jail in St. Ann on October 3. *(Photo by Russell Kinsaul/KMOV)*

Protestors celebrate after release from jail in St. Ann, where they had been transferred after being arrested in Ferguson while protesting. *(Photo by Robert Cohen/St. Louis Post-Dispatch/Polaris)*

Activist Jamell Spann during a protest march. *(Photo by Kenny Bahr/KFB Photography)*

CHAPTER 5

Where Have All the Leaders Gone?

"Now that you have touched the women, you have struck a rock,
you have dislodged a boulder, you will be crushed."

South African Women's Freedom Song

One of the questions that has routinely arisen since Michael Brown was killed is, "Where are the leaders?" Folks near and far questioned the "validity" of the movement because they didn't see any "leaders." Cable news pundits, celebrities and commoners alike spouted skepticism about the viability of this movement for racial justice because they didn't see any leaders or perceive any leadership. Sometimes it's hard to see what you're not looking for. There were no optics of a single person leading the masses toward the "promised land." No one person could be heralded as being in charge of the protests, and there was no spokesperson for the movement.

What emerged from the ground up was an eclectic group of people, many of them young, and most of them black women. The leaders of this new school of thought were too often unrecognizable because many in our society rarely conceive of them as leaders. . In this chapter, women leaders give voice to the ways in which leadership emerged in this movement and the centrality of the role of women.

Karen Anderson, the pastor of Ward Chapel AME Church in Florissant, Missouri, makes a case for how she sees the distinctiveness of women's leadership in this movement and sees parallels to the overlooking of women's leadership in the church.

At this time in history there's a strong need for a woman's voice There's strength in a woman's voice but it's tinged with compassion and understanding and a desire to move to a place of resolution. I think women aren't so entrenched in being right. I think we're more entrenched in ending with a right outcome. We don't have to be right. But we want the right outcome. And we're very clear about what the outcome is.

I think there's a need for a woman's voice because of the lens that we look through. We even interpret scripture differently, and I think that, many times, women see the people whose voices we don't hear in scripture as clearly and so we don't preach the text like everybody else preaches it.

So I think that's why women's voices, right now, are powerful. I think it's also the reason God is calling women in leadership in this movement, in the young women and even in clergy, but I also think it's the pushback that society has right now. And it's why they're saying there's no leadership—because it doesn't look like what they're used to. And it's the same; it can be the same within the church, and with the black church where you would think we would understand. It's the same. Women voices in the black church have also been disregarded the same way, saying there's no leadership.

For decades, black womanist and feminist scholars have rendered critical critique of the role of black women in the church and society, and called attention to the need to dismantle sexist and racist practices that too often render black women second-class citizens. In her book titled *If It Wasn't for the Women,* sociologist Dr. Cheryl Townsend Gilkes explores the multiple roles of black women in the church, family, and community; and the ways in which their contributions have been indispensible to the well-being and sustainability of families and communities.[1] Gilkes brought to the forefront the role of women as the "backbone" of churches and communities, yet often undervalued by patriarchal systems that denied them official leadership roles, so

---

[1]Cheryl Townsend Gilkes, *If It Wasn't for the Women: Black Women's Experience and Womanist Culture in Church and Community* (Maryknoll, N.Y.: Orbis Books, 2001).

that they were left to find creative ways to make their voices heard. Ethicist Keri Day issues the challenge for black churches to not only celebrate the "backbone" sacrifices of African American women, but to acknowledge the need for the church to stand in solidarity with poor black women and help dismantle the social injustices that threaten their economic stability.[2]

Black Lives Matter

The #blacklivesmatter motto emerged in 2013 shortly after George Zimmerman was found "not guilty" of the second degree murder charge in the killing of Trayvon Martin. Patrisse Cullors and Alicia Garza engaged in a Facebook conversation about the message it sent to black people that a person could kill an unarmed black teenager and not be held accountable. On February 26, 2012, George Zimmerman called 911 from his car in Sanford, Florida, because he saw a young man who "...looks like he's up to no good, he's on drugs or something." He went on to justify this call by saying, "It's raining and he's just walking around, looking about."[3] We now know that Zimmerman was referring to Trayvon Martin, the 17-year -old who was merely walking home from the store.

As Martin continues walking, Zimmerman says "These a*******, they always get away." Unfortunately, the phone call and Zimmerman's actions do not end here. Zimmerman proceeded to ensure that this "a*******" did not "get away". He got out of his car, ran after Martin, a scuffle ensued and ended with Zimmerman shooting and killing Martin in "self-defense." A jury agreed that Zimmerman's lethal actions were justified, all charges were dismissed, and his gun was returned to him.

Cullors and Garza, like many black people in the United States, felt the sting of yet another homicide that was fraught with racially charged rhetoric and antics. Many cable news pundits and radio talk show hosts set out to assassinate Trayvon Martin's character by describing him as a "thug" and intimating he deserved this fate. It was an attempt to dehumanize Martin, because once you dehumanize someone in the minds of others, it is a lot easier for them to accept inhumane treatment of that person (or persons). When Cullors and Garza decided to affirm

---

[2]Keri Day, *Unfinished Business: Black Women, the Black Church and the Struggle to Thrive in America* (Maryknoll, N.Y.: Orbis Books, 2012).

[3]http://news.blogs.cnn.com/2012/03/20/911-calls-paint-picture-of-chaos-after-florida-teen-is-shot/ Accessed February 1, 2015.

the value of black lives with the term #blacklivesmatter, it soon found a home on social media and beyond. To say that #blacklivesmatter is to (1) see black people as human beings and not racist stereotypes; (2) affirm the human dignity and value of black people as equal to all other people; and (3) challenge the hearer or reader to consider what it means to create a social order that values the lives of black people in all facets of their existence.

The initiators of the #blacklivesmatter crusade called forth a reimagining of society—one in which black lives are respected and black people are "seen as the powerful, beautiful, brilliant, talented, innovative, resourceful, creative folks that we are."[4] This type of visionary and creative action is consistent with the ways in which leadership has emerged throughout the movement for racial justice in Ferguson. Even though the #blacklivesmatter ideal was presented *before* Michael Brown was killed, many of the respondents to his killing quickly grabbed hold of the #blacklivesmatter slogan because it embodied the essence of what they were responding to.

For many, they were responding to the fact that an 18-year-old, unarmed, young black man was killed in the middle of the day, in the middle of a main apartment thoroughfare, and his body lay in the street for over four hours. It was the ultimate expression of disregard for black life, so the gravitation to the #blacklivesmatter slogan was an appropriate fit.

The women who launched the #blacklivesmatter initiative, as well as the women who have provided leadership during the movement for racial justice in Ferguson, are all emblematic of the ways in which leadership is taking shape in today's world. The "one size fits all" and "top down" approach does not resonate with the young activists of today, and it is incumbent upon the rest of us to look more closely at how they are providing leadership in creative and innovative ways.

Brittany Ferrell, one of the founders of Millennial Activists United, offers a candid description of how she understands leadership to have emerged in this movement.

When people think leader, they think it should be one singular individual who's charismatic enough to galvanize the nation. But what they have now is a charismatic group of individuals all over the nation who partake in group-centered leadership because,

---

[4]Blacklivesmatter.tumblr.com accessed on March 15, 2015.

when one person has to attend to their life as it goes on within the movement or as one person makes mistakes or as one person goes through the ups and downs of life, the movement continues, it carries on.

It's all a part of the love and support that's engrained in the movement. With group-centered leadership, why, you're able to support one another because we all have the same goal in mind. We're working at different paces and we're all working on. It's like this big clock. And each group or each individual is working on an important piece to contribute to making those hands turn; those hands are black life. Those hands are black freedom and black liberation. Those are those hands, and we've got to get those hands to turn, right? But for those hands to turn, we've got to have people advocating for all black lives, gay, straight, whatever.

We have to have people advocating for equality in education. We've got to have people who are trying to end this "cradle to prison" pipeline. We've got to have people who are going to challenge this prison industrial complex. We have to have people who are going to advocate for equal healthcare for poor people—poor, black people.

It's many different gears that we have to work on to get this— these hands of this clock to move. And each gear is working. Each gear is working. It's not worried about the next gear. It's working on what it's got to do to work. It's doing its work. This one's doing its work.

So if one of those gears says, "I'm getting a promotion. I'm out of here, right—people want to get into politics now because they are done building their platform. People want to move out of the city that they were fighting in because they got a greater following, and they got a better opportunity somewhere else. If one of those gears up and leaves, what's going to happen? Those clocks—the hands on that clock are never going to move.

So that is group-centered leadership. That's how you make it work for a community. You have an understanding that you're working together. It's not about, "Hey, I'm on this pedestal," "I'm the next MLK," because what you saw was not MLK. What you did not see was Ella Baker. What you saw was not Malcolm X. What you did not see is: who was holding [Malcolm X's] head when he was shot and killed? A woman, an Asian woman.

So it's like you see the iconic leadership that they want to portray to you in this individualized society, but you don't see all the workings behind it. Who wants to follow queer black women? Who wants to follow this unrespectable, tattooed, pierced up, sagging pants black man? Who wants to follow a rapper? Anybody, I feel like, who wants to criticize the leadership that is emerging within this movement—you cannot have been here to see it with your own two eyes. You cannot be paying attention, or...you are and your perception of what leadership is is skewed. MLK had a doctoral degree. Yeah, that's great, but this is a whole different generation. We're still working on the same thing you all were working on then. So being respectable has gotten us how far? So leadership is present. It's here. It's working, and... we're going to continue to do things the way that we've been doing it and we're going to continue to do it in a Godlike manner and we're going to continue to do it unapologetically so.

Karen Yang, a young adult activist and seminary student, builds on the ideas about how leadership has emerged through young people in this movement. This current movement for racial justice has often been compared to the Civil Rights Movement of the 1960s. Yang juxtaposes what she sees as some of the ways in which leadership ideals have emerged since then, and the role of women leading out front instead of being behind the scenes.

I think, from a very early age, I knew that feminist and woman rights issues were really important to me. My parents are immigrants from Taiwan, and I think there are some holdovers of patriarchy in that, and this is not to say that's just a Taiwanese issue. America has so many issues with patriarchy and, like, male supremacy as well, but it's manifested in a different way. And so, because of heritage, I think, I was more attuned to how inequality—whether it's gender or economic or racial— can really ruin people's lives and they can, like, literally be life threatening. And so that was part of why I got involved with

Faith Aloud [agency] in the first place, and, then, when I went to SisterSong [Reproductive Justice Conference], it really woke me up in the sense of I never heard, in that way before, how social justice can combine with reproductive rights, how gender issues can intersect with racial and ethnic issues.

So going to SisterSong was also the same year that I went to a conference called PANAAWTM. It's a conference for Asian and Asian American women in theology and ministry in North America. And that was when I really started to wake up to the importance of actually being Asian, I think. When I grew up, I was in a predominantly Asian and Asian American community and so I hadn't really experienced white supremacy to the way that it has manifested in Missouri. I think there definitely was still white supremacy, but it's more in the sense of like when people try to assimilate in America as a way of surviving and noticing that Asians and Asian Americans aren't necessarily in positions of leadership. But that wasn't something I actually really thought about or discovered until really recently, actually.

Growing up in that environment, I didn't actually think that it was very important to be Asian. I thought it was just a fact, and I thought racism was just people not being very smart or educated and so I only really experienced it as maybe my mom and my sister and I would be in a car and then another car of speeding white teenagers would drive by and they'd yell like just words—just sounds as if like speaking Chinese. You know, that "ching, chong," whatever stuff. And so, to me, I was always like, "That's so dumb," and I always defined myself as my personality, and I never really thought of the impact of my race or ethnicity, or didn't really think that it was important.

So the reason why I got involved to the extent that I did with everything surrounding the racial equality movement, coming out of Ferguson to the extent that I did was it was just all the pieces were coming together for me at that time. The importance of racial equality and how that works was something that matters to me at my deepest core, just equality of people in general.

I was really starting to understand my place in the world and my role as I was talking to a friend, and she said, "Karen, in all this that was happening with Michael Brown, you are the next best thing to white." And so, that was a statement really to illustrate and highlight that I cannot just see myself as a minority, as someone who is just equal with—in terms of treatment—with African Americans because of the model minority myth that has been used as a wedge between East Asians like myself and between other people of color, particularly brown-skinned people and people with black skin. That has been used as a wedge...to have people who look like me believe that we are somehow better, that our health is better, that our test scores and academics are better, that we perform better in the workplace and we deserve all of these things.

This is a way of driving us apart and discouraging us from being in solidarity with our kin who are also people of color who do not benefit from white supremacy, and our being hurt and our dying from it. And so all of this has really woken me up and there's this hashtag, "Stay woke advent," that popped up for theology of Ferguson, and I think that's really true. I've really felt woken up to the position that I hold in society, and I have a choice. I have a choice to assimilate with the demands and expectations of white supremacy, to be a good model minority; and, instead, I want to choose and to take inspiration from the other people who insist and wear shirts even as they do actions around immigration reform or things like that—not your model minority. We are not going to be your Asian sidekick. We're not going to uphold white supremacy just in hopes that we might get a little bit of the benefit for ourselves just so that we might survive ourselves— just so that, after all that we've done...

The beloved community is a term that Martin Luther King, Jr., brought to popularity, and it's this idea that everyone should be able to—should treat each other like family. We should care for each other like family, and agape love, which is the love that seeks to preserve and create community, should be the norm... And I think that's something that has parallels today because we are rewriting history right now, and if you want to talk about what Millennials are like—when I look at the young activists right now, what Millennials are like are people who have learned from people like Martin Luther King, Jr., and the other forbearers of our Civil Rights Movement and then put a twist on it. They're saying, "We don't need a charismatic leader like Martin Luther King, Jr.," even though people...in the public, in their everyday lives are saying, "Where are the leaders?"

I hear from my classmates sometimes. They're confused, and they want to know who the leaders are that can answer for us, and the thing is, with the growth of coalitions, I think that's a beautiful good thing. And it's not to say that there is no leadership. It just means that we are realizing hierarchy does not work for us. Kyriarchy is not working for us. Collaboration is what will work. The beloved community, where we're all holding hands and marching together, where we're linking arms and marching together on the same level—that is what will work, where our reverends are not in our pulpits up high anymore and, if they are, that they're coming down and climbing down to be with the people. That is what will work.

Now we're seeing a difference in leadership, and that's a good thing, I think. And even if you see that there are statements from these different coalitions, they're doing that on the fly. And when I was a part of coalition work, I was seeing that happen all the time—so many e-mails, countless e-mails going back and forth immediately after any event happened, immediately responding with a press conference to tell the press, "This is our stance. These are our demands." And you can look it up—websites cropping up all over, saying, "These are the protestors' demands. These are the Don't Shoot Coalition's demands. These are the Praying with Our Feet Clergy Coalition demands."

And some people might look at that and feel that it's scattered and disorganized, but I look at that and see there are threads throughout these demands. People are talking to each other. People don't do this perfectly, but it's beautiful that collaboration and cooperation is the norm rather than hierarchy. So, whether that's online, in spur of the moment responses to different actions, or just creating different ideas of thought for people to chew on, they're also working with coalitions to create those official-looking responses of unity documents or demands or press conferences. And they know that they're not always being heard, so they need to express themselves in a variety of ways, and they're also not afraid to shake people up because it's more about really galvanizing and waking up the public than about appealing to people already in power, because they know that appealing to people already in power does not work and has not worked, which is why we are in this situation.

Another difference I see with the Millennial movements for activism is a difference in who's allowed to be leadership. So you see people who are activists who are also uplifting different leaders—like, really uplifting woman leaders in the movement and recognizing that, even though our memory says that our Civil Rights Movement was led "by well-dressed black men who were reverends," that there were really strong woman leaders who were not just behind it but also leading.

What they mean is that, when people are trying to shame protestors or activists for not looking a certain way, for not speaking a certain way…for using profanity, for not dressing as nicely, for not having as much of a deference to authority, for not always going through the so-called proper channels of making change, that people grow impatient with that and—or that people shame others for that. And their response is that, in the previous Civil Rights Movement, even though protests were, by their nature, not accepted, there was more respectability in the sense that people did try to dress nice. People were extremely committed to nonviolence—even though they are still committed to nonviolence today, of course. And I don't want to—of course but it—it's—that hasn't changed. But what has changed is that people are not so willing to think that dressing a certain way or speaking a certain way will make a difference because they know that what they have to say is being expressed, and they are expressing in multiple ways.

Dietra Wise Baker is the pastor of Liberation Christian Church in St. Louis. She picks up the theme of comparison to the Civil Rights Movement and an additional perspective of the ways clergy have emerged as leaders in this movement.

The idea of one leader or methodology, that's dead. The work is too heavy. The work is too heavy and too multifaceted for one charismatic leader. There needs to be a letting go of that, a letting go of needing to be "the one" for us, for us being "the one." That's been a deep, painful, but good spiritual and vocational lesson—that this work is work that we do together, that this never was work that "I do alone" or in a silo.

But I think some had a vision of leadership, particularly when it came to the community, that one charismatic leader would emerge, and that's how it was going to happen. And there have been lots of leaders who have emerged, and maybe some people say there is one, but the reality is there isn't. There are many leaders. There are theological leaders. There are activist leaders. There are people who are doing both. There are people who are bridging. There's all kind of work that has to be done, and there are all kinds of people doing it.

Karen Yang reads a lament on Moral Monday at the Ferguson police station. *(Photo by Vanessa Myers-Dudley)*

Traci Blackmon uses a megaphone to talk to a large group of demonstrators August 14, 2014 at the site where Michael Brown, Jr. was shot and killed. *(AP photo)*

CHAPTER 6

This Is What Theology Looks Like

"If our church is not marked by caring for the poor, the oppressed, the hungry, we are guilty of heresy."

St. Ignatius of Loyola

Caring for people who are oppressed and disenfranchised is a core tenet of many religious faiths. Oftentimes, faith communities express their care by donating food and clothes to those in need, sending teams on mission trips to provide resources in underserved countries, and donateing money to organizations that provide these kinds of services. These are vital and important resources that faith communities can and should provide; however, there is yet another element of caring for the oppressed that should not be overlooked: doing justice. To do justice for the oppressed is to *correct* the injustice that is being done, not to only provide a balm for the hurts that have been caused. To do justice *is* to care for the oppressed, and to stand in solidarity with the oppressed is to oppose the injustices thrust upon them.

For many clergy who responded to the killing of Michael Brown, their rationale was deeply tied to their understanding of God and the mission of the church. They preached about the ill effects of racism upon young black men, held book discussions about bias in the criminal justice system with Michelle Alexander's *The New Jim Crow*, and provided community lectures as part of Metropolitan Congregations United's sacred conversations on race. There was not a separation between faith and justice, but their faith in God was expressed through their acts of doing justice. For these clergy, to stand with the oppressed is to stand with God. To correct injustices in the world that oppress is to work with God. To journey with people through the valley of injustice toward creating a future filled with hope is to walk with God.

Dietra Wise Baker is a chaplain for the St. Louis County juvenile detention center and the pastor of Liberation Christian Church (DOC) in St. Louis. She connects her experiences as a chaplain with what she witnessed as a Ferguson responder, and relates it to the work of the congregations.

> For me, because...the environment that I work in is with juveniles—mostly African American girls and boys in this particular context—Mike Brown's body is still on the ground. For all intents and purposes, in the context that I serve in every day, Mike's body is still on the ground. So in terms of doing the work and being motivated for it, I was pulling on all those kids whose certification hearings I sat in and feeling this nagging question from God, "When are you going to do something about this besides sitting here and being present for the certification hearing and offer support and prayers as they go off to prison?" So somewhere deep inside me, I felt like this is the beginning of what I needed to get me passionate. I always was, but it was like a match got lit. Something got lit being out in the streets with the young people, knowing all the stuff they're talking about, knowing and understanding theologically and contextually all of the issues. But the kids that I sit with every day, the black and brown faces of girls and boys that I'm around every day, this became like some kind of spark of saying—Mike speaking to me in a way, like, "I'm still on the ground, Dietra," and seeing his face in my kids and understanding that there's a lot of work that needs to be done to get him off the ground.

For Dietra, the work of "getting him off the ground" extended beyond just providing prayer and support to the youth in juvenile detention. She understood that her work for justice had to include actions of care that sought to correct injustices that contribute to these youths' incarceration. Her work also extended into the congregation, Liberation Christian Church, where she regularly framed issues of injustice as social *and* theological issues. She says:

For [Liberation Christian Church], it wasn't a new conversation. Liberation has always had a context in liberation theology and understanding how systems of power work and how they oppress. And so there was already a framework that was easy to preach from and work with. Some of them were out in the street more than I was. They kind of have their own way of being present as liberators in the world. They understand their identity in that way theologically, and so they understood, clearly, when this happened, that this is a place that we need to be present.

We liberate lives and communities, and so we need to be present in the community at this moment. The pastor doesn't need to beg us or call us or tell us when to show up or anything of that kind of stuff. They knew the information. They were present at the meetings. Sometimes, they were informing me of stuff. So theologically, there was already a foundation in the life of our church for people to really own the community as part of their identity, and, in our church, people do own the community as part of our own identity as a church. And so there was no pleading or prodding or problems with me preaching about it on anything like that. People just got more fired up, usually. In our context, community liberation, black people, racism, sexism, heterosexism are given places of critique, and they're not really troubling critiques in our context. This kind of work is a part of who we are as a church.

Dietra is also the Clergy Caucus co-chair for Metropolitan Congregations United along with Samuel Voth Schrag, pastor of St. Louis Mennonite Fellowship, and was responsible for inviting other local clergy to participate in Ferguson-related responses. Some clergy were just not interested, others chose not to participate out of fear of repercussions from their congregations, while some participated knowing the risk involved.

I didn't get the calls, letters, and e-mails that some of my colleagues had to deal with around preaching about Ferguson and being on the streets. I know that there are some pastors who kind of stepped aside from their congregation to at least be in conversation with those of us who are active, so that they could engage a little bit. But I kept challenging when things were really, really hot. I said, "Just get on the streets. Come be on the streets. Come at least once. Get on the streets. I'm telling you you're going to meet Jesus there. Jesus on the street and you're going to be transformed if you come to the street. You can't be transformed in the safety of the pew and at the church. And I know that you're afraid, and I know you're wondering what people are going to say, think. You're wondering what's going to happen when you get out there. I get it. On some level, I've experienced that, but come to the street and then you will see what we mean, and you'll be transformed."

Moral Monday

One of the biggest displays of clergy protesting in the streets was on Monday, October 13. The event was titled "Moral Monday," and culminated the end of weekend-long resistance efforts under the umbrella of "Ferguson October." Moral Monday was a call for clergy to give voice to the systemic injustices and frame them as a moral and ethical issue that plagues our nation. The event was similar to the Moral Monday efforts led by William Barber and a coalition of faith-based and social justice groups in North Carolina that confronted legislative acts that negatively impacted poor and minority people.

Hundreds of people marched from Wellspring Church to the Ferguson police station and rallied there despite the rainstorm. Some clergy approached police officers and offered prayers, others were arrested as a show of solidarity with the cause for justice. Shaun Jones, assistant pastor of Mt. Zion Baptist Church Complex in St. Louis, drew theological meaning out of the symbolism of marching in the rain for the cause of justice.

The day when it was pouring down rain in front of the Ferguson police station on Moral Monday, there were clergy from all over the city, white and black, men and women, and to hear 400 people or so singing "Wade in the Water" was a powerful moment for me. I've sung that song at many baptism services in my life, but I understood that day what it really meant to wade in the water. While I wasn't in a river, a pool, or a lake, I was wading in the water toward justice. I felt the water beating on our heads and our faces, but we were determined that we were not going to be moved. We were going to be steadfast and unmovable, as the Bible says, at that moment of accomplishment.

Sara Herbertson, an Episcopal Service Corp intern from Connecticut, describes her experience of that event:

It was the torrential downpour day where we were singing "Wade in the Water" really intensely. It was so incredible, and I remember up until that point, I hadn't felt the pull or the total desire and, like, a true, real, raw way to just jump and be ready to be taken down, like incarcerated.

We were on the ground praying with our director at the time, literally face to the ground, and the riot police were right there. And we're like, all right, jump through and be taken in through their legs, that was the idea and – to make that statement. And it just felt right, and we did it, and we were soaked the entire day in jail. And I recall very vividly, in the backseat of the police van, they allowed us to keep our phones, and I called my mom. And she's like, "Oh, God. Does it go on your record?"

But it was one of those experiences that was just shockingly enlightening and just, like, really incredible and that I was with all these other women that – it happened – that were all really upbeat. And we were singing in our cell, and we were making it a good experience somehow. And it was really interesting, and we even discussed something with an inmate that was there. It was just like – he was brought to the light sort of. He was happier just being around us, and considering the circumstances he was in, that was impressive.

Basically, I experienced the coming together of all people of so many different walks of life, and I had never witnessed something like that. It was just inexplicably powerful, of course. But it felt historical, and not many people can necessarily say that they were there for that. So it hits you later, but that was how I did. I just jumped in.

Millennial Activists United co-founder Alexis Templeton describes the police disposition on Moral Monday as radically different than the other times they had encountered the police during protests. Once again, she connects their action to being reflective of the mission of the church.

> Even during the clergy march [on Moral Monday]...the police, like, man, they were just chilling. There was no hardness on them because you had people like Rabbi Susan. You had your Nelsons [Pierce] standing at the front of all this... That became their pulpit right there. Standing on the frontlines was their pulpit. You brought the church to the Ferguson Police Department. You became that church. It's like they were standing in front of pews in riot gear. You just had an abundance of prayer going around... It was dope.

Nelson Pierce, a St. Louis native who is currently a pastor in Ohio, articulates his participation in the movement as being explicitly linked to his Christian identity. For Pierce, participation in the Moral Monday clergy march (among many other protests) was reflective of the biblical prophets' role to hold those in power accountable for their actions upon the people.

> I believe it's the call of God throughout biblical history and even today, and so I was saying the kings, when the kings of Israel fell short of that, that God sent prophets to call them back to that. And I even think that even in the life, in the ministry of Jesus, what made it such a powerful force in its time and what made it such a threat to the Roman Empire was that it was more than just a spiritual movement or calling, but it was a calling to reimagine life under [Roman rule]. [The message was that] that life, as the way the Romans prescribed it, wasn't all there was, that God was actually calling for a new way of living and being a community together that resisted oppression.
>
> And so, I have become increasingly convinced that, at least for me, I cannot be a Christian if I am not actively engaged in the dismantling of oppression where I live and helping the dismantling

of oppression around the world. That is part of what it means to me to be a follower of Jesus Christ.

Several clergy used their relationships, status, and strength for the benefit of the young people to say to the police and to the justice system "These are our people, and we are going to work to get them [out of jail during protests]. That was important for the young people to see. I think it was important for the clergy, too, in helping cement for them the importance of this relationship. It was also important for the police and others to see that these young people were not without support. But the most important thing isn't just getting to know them, but how are we using our strength and institutional resources on behalf of them?

Pierce goes on to describe a conversation with a young activist who questioned the value of the church to young people if it is not addressing the issues that negatively impact young people.

And so he said, "What the young people are feeling is we're out here, and we have to fight all of these adults, and the church ought to be the people who are fighting the adults with us or for us, and they're not. Instead, we're getting harassed and mistreated and shot and killed by the police and then the church turns to us and says, 'Well, you need to pull up your pants,' or, 'You need to be more respectable and that will change things,' rather than go to the police and say, 'Hey, stop messing with our kids.' And so I'm just waiting for somebody to come out and say to the police, 'Stop messing with our kids.'"

So I think that's the lesson out of this…, not just in terms of resources but also our theology, our preaching—that, if we're not using the resources, the theological and prophetic resources of the church, in ways that call attention to the injustice and speak truth to the power of the broken police system and the broken criminal justice system in America, then how do we expect our young people, who are facing these struggles every day, to believe in the church?

Beyond Hospitality

The questions that Ferguson has raised for congregations have also pricked the consciousness of those within some of the religious educational institutions in St. Louis. The call to do justice echoed within the halls of Eden Theological Seminary, and the protestors even landed on the doorstep of St. Louis University.

Eden Seminary's academic dean, Deborah Krause, is an ordained Presbyterian clergyperson. She was actively engaged in the street protests in Ferguson, while thinking about the meaning of this work for the institution as well. The idea of standing with the protestors is not limited to faith communities alone, but is consistent with the ethos of other religious-based institutions of higher education.

One of the biggest shifts in how I think about theological education and the role of the seminary since Ferguson has come in how I think of the school in relationship to racism. I have always been clear—along with the faculty—that Eden as an institution of Euro-American heritage is racist. We have felt called to work on and dismantle our structural racism. We've worked at access to racial-ethnic minority students and in particular in the St. Louis region to black students. We've committed resources to scholarships, faculty development, and we've delved into course content. All of this has been important, and we have seen an increase in our black student enrollment to over 25 percent. This is something we have rightly worked hard at and celebrated.

And yet, I think my imagination has really been focused on how that is about "hospitality." It has been about being welcoming to students of color and being relevant to the black church. We have focused on the student experience—how can Eden be more welcoming? How can Eden be a school that black students could celebrate as their school? So the focus has been on access, welcome, relevance, and hospitality. But since Ferguson, there has been an important shift, and I can't not see it this way anymore, and that has been toward figuring out how the seminary can be an agent in the movement of dismantling racism in the church and broader community. Of course, this doesn't mean we stop working on our own racism, but it puts that project in the service of a much bigger sense of mission. What would it mean for us to see this school as an agent of dismantling racism, and an agent of confronting and combatting white supremacy?

One story in our history gets at this ambivalence on race in a powerful way. When I first joined the faculty at Eden in 1992 I remember learning that the seminary was the first Euro-American institution of higher learning in Missouri to admit a person of color. That was in 1932. That fact was shared with me as a part of the heroic history of the school as an agent of social transformation, and I was proud of it. I have over the years pointed out to friends and colleagues at SLU and Wash. U. that their schools (in 1945 and 1958 respectively) began to integrate decades after Eden.

In 1932 Eden admitted an AME pastor named Joseph Gomez to its STM program, the first black student admitted to a white graduate school in the state of Missouri. Since Ferguson, however, I have had the chance to do some reading that has somewhat clouded this heroic history of the seminary for me. Turns out that Rev. Gomez was admitted at Eden, but only after he had first been denied. According to Gomez's biography, written by his wife, Joseph and the local chapter of the NAACP identified the seminary as a good candidate for testing desegregation on the basis of its mission statement. At the time, Eden had a mission that read something like: "Eden Seminary…is a school open to students of all Christian denominations." So Gomez, on the basis of that mission statement, applies, and he's rejected. And I think he probably knew he would be because it's a white segregated institution. So anyway, he was denied.

That little detail was left out when I first heard the story, but it is such an amazing part of it, because Gomez and the NAACP went on a letter-writing campaign in the *St. Louis Argus* and church publications pressuring the school to admit him because the mission statement says "open to students of all Christian denominations," and this is a student of a Christian denomination. So what is preventing you? At that point, the faculty reconsiders and admits him in 1932. So he graduates two years later with a STM.

Now this kind of strategic social pressure seems like a foreshadowing of the kinds of challenges to segregation that led tweny years later up to Brown vs. Board of Education. It's like a precursor to the landmark desegregation act in our nation's history, and Eden is a part of that history. As it turns out we were a reluctant part in that history. It was our vocation, embodied in that mission statement that bore the seeds of our redemption, that paved the way for Gomez and others to call the seminary out of its sinfulness to join the human freedom movement. And this has helped me see the ambivalence of the seminary towards its role in the human freedom movement. We are at once culturally reluctant and vocationally summoned beyond our acculturated horizon. That is who we are. It's far from heroic, and it should always alert us to the need of God's grace in the witness of our sisters and brothers who suffer and who are in the struggle.

Recently in a Board of Trustees strategic planning meeting with the faculty, I told this story about Gomez to the group at my table. We were talking about our vision and mission and I offered that I think we need to state very openly that we are an anti-white supremacist, antiracist institution, because who knows what horizon of our acculturation we're not seeing today. If we claim that we are an antiracist and anti-white supremacist school we will need to move from that old comfortable idea of "how can we be more welcoming and hospitable" to black students and people of color. It's not like I am beating myself up about that stance, but, if we understand that we are vocationally engaged in the human freedom movement, then what we're doing is not just trying to be welcoming to our African American students. We're working to engage all our students, faculty, and staff (white, black, and brown) as agents of transformation, as agents of anti-white supremacy, as agents of antiracism, as agents of human freedom in their leadership in church and society.

White supremacy is idolatry. Every part of the tradition of this school, from the evangelical German and reformed heritage to the faculty's current liberation and postcolonial theological perspectives hates idolatry. So if we hate idolatry and we say we want to create transformational leaders, what kinds of transformation are we talking about? The transformation is of this society. The transformation is of us, of the people. What needs to be transformed is our sinfulness and our brokenness, which is expressed socially, systemically, most pointedly, I think, in our context in this time as white supremacy and structural racism. This is the summons of our vocation in our place and time. It is the work God is calling us to be about as a school and as a church.

So I guess that's what I see has changed for me with regard to thinking about theological education. Ferguson is a great unveiling of the extent of the systemic evil of racism in our community. We knew at many levels that much was wrong, but many of us had become dull in our ability to hear and understand the suffering of black people in St. Louis. And this has rung the bell for me. I believe now that this is what we're here for. This is our calling. And, in the process, what's happened for me over the past three or four months is that I have found myself in interfaith work like I've never been before. I found myself in intercultural dialogue and work on antiracism like I've never been before. These are all things I said I cared about before, but now I'm actually doing them. It's like I am being re-humanized. And I think our colleagues on the faculty would agree—God is really working on us now! In that, I think, the school is vitalized. I know I am vitalized. I believe the church is vitalized. So I think this is our window of time for the Seminary to live into its vocation, its life, its purpose.

The problem of racism is huge—it touches everything. It touches on every aspect of what it means to be human. And it covers every dimension: from unconscious and conscious beliefs to the structure of society. So the resources of a school like Eden with all our capacity to do systemic, theological analysis and structural analysis as well as personal, spiritual work—we're the kind of a school that can open ourselves up to this movement, be shaped by this movement, and maybe in the process even be a resource for this movement. Far from a center that welcomes people in, it seems like this metaphor of the movement is helping me to see the Seminary as an agent through which God's purposes are flowing—if we can just have the faith to open up and join in.

Occupy St. Louis

The call to "join in" came quite loudly to the doorstep of St. Louis University on October 13, when one of the school courtyards was occupied with protestors. Alisha Sonnier is a St. Louis University student and one of the founders of Tribe X activist group. The group emerged from the Ferguson protests, and their focus is on educating and organizing. After protestors occupied St. Louis University, Alisha was one of the driving forces who forged conversations with the administration about racism on campus, as well as the need for using university resources to help improve community conditions.

When you talk about Occupy SLU, that was something that we got very strategic out of that. Now we have the Clock Tower Accords. Now we're having conversation with the university, and we have resources that will hopefully reach the community that are being worked on. And those are meetings that I go to on a regular basis. Those are meetings that our advisors go to on a regular basis. Those are meetings that other Tribe X members go to on a regular basis to help those resources get out there.

Tribe X came to be from a group of people we met. So after the first night in Ferguson, we went out there so many more times. You ran into a lot of people you often saw there, a lot of familiar faces. You had a lot of similar conversations. We started talking, and we decided to have some meetings. We went to our meetings, and we were just talking about ways that we could be effective, and we were just tired of just talking about it and complaining about it, but we wanted to figure out, "What could we do?"

And so it was actually suggested to us by one of our advisors, "Well, why don't you guys start an organization?" And we talked about it, and we tried to weigh the benefits of an organization. And, it was a more disciplined way to go about what we wanted to do. We started talking about our roots and where we came from. The issue came up, and we were talking about police and slavery and things like that. The only thing that we really knew for certain about Africa and that we thought we could assume about ourselves is that we probably came from some tribe. We'll probably never know the tribe's name. So X is unknown, so Tribe X—kind of to stand for your unknown roots but trying to get back to who you really are, the origin and the content of your soul, especially when it comes to black people.

We try to focus on empowerment. Another thing we're talking about is educating people on voting because we find that, if it's not the presidential election, people, if they do vote locally, they're going and, if they're Democrats, they're checking down a Democrat row. If they're Republican, they're checking down a Republican row, and I don't want to see that. I want to see some education happening. I want people to vote aware and so I guess next steps would be us focusing on that—those areas of the political structure, focusing on the Clock Tower Accords and making those things happen and to give back to the community and give back to minority students here on campus and possibly creating some programming that we're talking about and working on right now about taking high schoolers out to get registered to vote or talking to them about the importance of activism and using your voice and that, really, you're not different from me. You're no different from me. You have a voice, and you can use it in the same capacity in a way that I do.

Fred Pestello, the President of St. Louis University, reflects on the school's response to the occupation and its subsequent role in light of the school's Jesuit tradition:

So we found ourselves in the midst of a protest and an encampment for which there's no rulebook. They don't teach you how to do deal with that in president's school. What we did is we quickly gathered around the table—the senior leaders—and literally asked ourselves questions like: "What would Christ do? What would St. Ignatius do? What would Pope Francis do?" and decided that the only thing we had to rely upon to guide our actions are our values and our mission.

So we felt called to reflect upon what it is for which we stand and to make decisions with respect to how to act on that basis. So why is the academy one of our most enduring and important institutions? Because we're the place where the most compelling questions of the day are asked and answers are explored. The academy must be the space in which well-educated people and those learning from them come together to ask questions and pursue answers, wherever the truth leads us. And I think that, in moments like these, you see the academy respond in that way.

I'm quite proud of the fact that we have faculty here who are deeply engaged and have been engaged, well before the tragic events in Ferguson, in exploring the issues, which have come to the fore as a result of that tragedy. We need to continue to do that. Academies, I think increasingly, especially large research universities in urban areas, are serving as anchor institutions where they partner with leaders—be they governmental, political, civic leaders—to help the region address its needs.

So I think, across the university, people are more concerned about, focused upon, and engaged with the challenges we face, and I see that well beyond the borders of our campus. I think, if you look at the challenge of municipal fragmentation and all the consequences of that in terms of how these tiny municipalities are funded and the percentage of revenue that comes through traffic fines and so forth, we know we have a significant issue here that has to be addressed, which is interwoven with other issues: poverty, violence, injustice, racism. There are a whole confluence of factors, challenges for urban public schools, which are challenges in nearly every major metropolitan area.

So I don't think St. Louis is at all unique in the problems we face, but I do think we have an opportunity now because people are focused on these issues given what happened, given that we have a Ferguson Committee charged by the governor looking at this explicitly. I do think most of the people with whom I speak sincerely want to begin to address what are longstanding, very complex, very large challenges and begin to make a difference. It's not an easy path, but I hope that I personally, and our university as a whole, can participate with others in making this a better place to work and live.

Anthony Witherspoon, pastor of Washington Metropolitan African Methodist Episcopal Zion Church and Cornell Brooks, President of the NAACP lead "Journey for Justice" march to Jefferson City. *(Photo by Kile Brewer)*

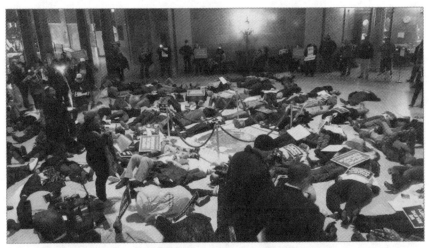

Activist Brittini Gray giving instructions during the "Die in" in the Capitol Rotunda in Jefferson City, January 7, 2015. *(Photo by Cassandra Gould)*

Jamal Bryant (AME, Baltimore), Traci Blackmon, Willis Johnson, Starsky Wilson, Waltrina Middleton (UCC national office), Iva Carruthers (Samuel Proctor Conference), Cornel West (Princeton) and Jim Wallis (Sojourners) participate in the Moral Monday march on October 13, 2014. *(Photo by Wiley Price/*St. Louis American*)*

Washington Tabernacle Baptist Church members ready to "pray with their feet" on August 17, 2014. *(Photo by Mitchell Hunter)*

Rally outside Greater St. Mark Family Church. *(Photo by Julie Taylor)*

CHAPTER 7

Why Are Your Doors Open to Us?

*"You can safely assume you've created God in your own image
when it turns out that God hates all the same people you do."*

Anne Lamott

The desire for belonging and acceptance is a basic human need, and young black people are no different than other people in having this desire. The fight for justice in this movement is a fight for the freedom to be seen and valued as human beings "just as you are"—not in a prescribed way that renders you acceptable so long as you fit a particular mold, but in an authentic way that makes room for each person to be able to be fully him- or herself. In chapter 4, Brittany Ferrell and Alexis Templeton raised important points about the role of intersectionality in the context of the Ferguson protests. They pointed to the convergence of demographics such as race, class, gender, sexuality, and age, as well as the intersectionality of social issues such as poverty, healthcare, and education. In this chapter, the stories of two pastors add to that conversation as they describe the ways in which their congregations became "safe sanctuaries" for a variety of people engaged in the Ferguson protests. They enlarged the concept of "safe sanctuary" to include both physical *and* emotional safety that can only occur when people are valued as full human beings, and not discriminated against because of their race, gender, class, or sexual orientation.

This Was a Gift to Us

Starsky Wilson is the pastor of St. John's UCC in north St. Louis and the CEO of the Deaconess Foundation. He describes how St. John's created "safe" space for the activists in the movement for racial justice.

I first learned of Michael Brown's death on August 9. I was at the church preparing for worship on Sunday, and I saw reports on Twitter, pictures of Mike Brown's stepfather holding up a sign that said that the police had just killed his son. And my most immediate reaction was to process a little bit with a couple of church members. That night, I went to my office here at Deaconess Foundation, and I reached into a box of books that I had, copies of Gregory Ellison's *Cut Dead but Still Alive,* and grabbed about 25 or 30 of them and took them with me to the church the next day, placed them on the altar, and they were on the altar during worship. I framed this responsibility for the church because we have lots of young boys in our church and suggested that we needed to do some critical reflection on how we care for them as much as we call others to care for them. And I remember, uniquely that day, we had a representative from St. Louis Public Schools there to talk about kids coming out on the first day of school, being present for the first day of school. And, on that day, we offered that everyone in the church who worked with kids and everyone who was in our Sunday school, anyone who's in our Sunday school leadership, youth leadership, or were educators and worked with kids needed to take a book. They committed to reading it and giving a two-page reflection on how it should change how we do Christian education and youth ministry at the church, and they were to turn those in to me before the second Sunday in September, because the second Sunday in September we would have members of "Jack and Jill" coming to be with us for their annual commemoration of the 16th Street bombing.[1]

[1] Jack and Jill of America, Inc. is a national organization of mothers dedicated to nurturing African American children for leadership in the 21st century. http://jackandjillinc.org/

St. John's UCC in St. Louis hosted two events of the #blacklivesmatter freedom ride—the first in early September and the second in October. Brittini Gray, a Millennial activist, seminary student, and church member, was struck by the witnessing of the diverse protest participants who came to the church, and likens it to a depiction of the kingdom of God.

Pastor Wilson has always been one to open the doors of the church for important matters, and so I don't even know what happened. I just looked up one day, and it was like, "Black Lives Matter is coming to town." And so, for the weekend, we became a host site providing shelter for people, providing space for strategy to take place, and providing a worship experience for them. That was probably the highlight of my year of worship, actually: to have them with us, to look around and see a sanctuary full of diverse people—and I mean diverse in all sense of race, of gender, of thought and belief and background. I had not been able to cry throughout the movement from when I heard about Michael Brown's death until the Black Lives Matter Sunday. Like I say, the diversity of the room, to me, it was a reflection of the kingdom of God. When we talk about people coming together in one accord, it had never been more apparent to me as it was in that moment, and it was just the most beautiful feeling I'd ever had. I think it was in that moment that I fell in love with the movement.

One of the things I talk about a lot with the church is that this movement is different. The church is still caught up in trying to be the next Civil Rights Movement and believing that we have the moral authority to lead a movement. And while I agree that there is a moral authority that comes from the church, this movement was not started by the church, and so we cannot claim something that we did not start. We can participate and sustain something, but we cannot claim it as if we are founders, because this is really a movement of the streets. It's a hip-hop movement. And so, as much as I am made and informed by the church, I am just as much made and informed by hip-hop as a culture. I live and I breathe it, and so, yes, I would have been engaged regardless because I grew up listening to Tupac and Biggie, to Common, to DeadPrez, to Eric B. and Rakim. I grew up on all of it. All of it which told me that the system was messed up, and I cannot listen to those lyrics, see those lyrics, internalize those lyrics, and not have a response when I outwardly see the system is messed up.

The Civil Rights Movement, as it concluded, created a very false reality for people and comfort in that while you still have social justice organizations and nonprofit work that was going on ... the majority of people really thought that we had arrived to a place that was good, and so, as a nation, we had been asleep. And what I saw here was an awakened people. What I felt was an awakened people who were coming together to call others to wake up, not just to be woke by ourselves and do the work in isolation, but to really put a call out. And that was one of the other things that was so beautiful about the gathering at St. John's is that you had people there from L.A., Atlanta, New York and everything in between, and, to me, that was one of the points where the movement spread and really began to take over the nation.

So I think that one of the things that the church can learn from the movement is how to be inclusive. What I love about the co-founders of Black Lives Matter, particularly Patrice [Cullors], is this adamant insistence that intersectionality matters and so it's not just about one issue or one type of person, but it's about holding together the complexities of human nature and life that create who we truly are. And so, until the church can wake up and understand that, then I don't know if I have too much hope. I think that's the greatest thing for us to learn.

Starsky Wilson reflects on the particular way St. John's opened to the freedom riders. Not only did they open the building, but they ensured that all could come without fear of being marginalized in any way.

Labor Day weekend, we get the call earlier that week that the Black Lives Matter freedom ride needs a place to gather for their teachings, to be a headquarters for their actions. We become that place at St. John's over the course of those four days that they're with us doing teach-ins, healing stations, organizing actions, reflecting. We become kind of their place.

When Ferguson October happens, they come back to us, and at our church they organize their week of resistance. So 200 people who came from the freedom ride come back. It was 450 people the first time. Two hundred people come back for Ferguson October and convene at the church in the basement, and there they organize, strategize a week of resistance that's to occur two weeks later. That's when you begin to see "Shut down the streets in Chattanooga," "Shut down the streets in Atlanta," "Shut down the BART in Oakland." That was organized in a church basement where the BLM riders come back and then they begin to trade ideas. Patrice is leading a group here. Ashley is leading a group there. Alexis and Brittany are leading a group over here, and they're breaking out and saying, "Okay. What are you all doing here? What could you all do?" And they're all learning and trading and networking with one another. So it's just the creation of space.

This has been my sixth year as pastor of St. John's and what I began to see is the church beginning to live out expressions of the theological hopes and asking, "How is it we've been preaching a beloved community, which includes this kind of multiethnic, multiracial community of peace and justice with love as the governing ethic, with this focus on a remarkable hospitality, if not a radical one, and not doing the work?" Not just engaging directly, but doing the work, and so some of that work is being open to others, and we began to see this. We saw this on the weekend of the BLM ride.

And so I said, "You know, everybody's welcomed to worship. Everybody doesn't do church. I understand that. So do what you want to do wherever—all over the building." But, and I think, out of just some deference and appreciation, some folks came to church who really don't do church. But, theologically, we began to preach. I recognized the responsibility here, particularly for this group that doesn't do church much, is to try, in their hearts and in their eyes, to represent a Christ that they can connect with and to redeem, in some ways, the representations that they may be familiar with and so that's what we do.

So that morning, we preached using the title from Obery Hendricks' *The Politics of Jesus,* and, quite frankly, using much of the theology from there, Jesus is radical revolutionary. And that tends to go over well with the group. They connect with that message. We see people responding to it. But it's also this reality that people who were there came up to us and said, "You let transgendered people in the church." And I didn't know how to respond to that. I was like, "What do you mean, '**let** somebody in church'?" But they had experienced that barrier, that boundary being set, that experience of being pushed out because of their orientation, because of how they show up, and so our church really became, for them, safe space and ground in St. Louis such that now we get asked, "Hey, can we come...we want to do this. We'd like to do it at St. John's."

One of the reasons this reflection is so compelling is because St. John's is a predominately black church that clearly embodies the belief that *all* black lives matter, and are governed by an ethic of love and hospitality. Starsky and Brittini clearly understand this diversity as a gift to the congregation and important to the faith. Instead of viewing diverse people as deficient, they, like all of the people I interviewed, view human diversity as a gift given to us by God. Starsky laments the loss of this gift to "the church" when they discriminate against people based on perceived difference.

I went to New York. I have a meeting with someone in this group of 450 people, and there are 12 Princeton seminary-trained and graduated young people. Six of whom are not engaged in church anywhere—because of the same matters: lack of hospitality, not feeling safe, not being connected. So I end up, when I go to New York, having a conversation in the subway station with a young man who's now discerning accepting an invitation to be ordained in the Reconciling Fellowship Churches in the UCC. But when he came, he wouldn't do church but he's considering it. So when you think about the spiritual capacity that the church has lost, because that kind of brilliance and call and deep faith that just can't do the tradition and refuses to show up with any less than his whole self.

That's the kind of remarkable opportunity this has been for us to be a church, and it has inspired others. So people in my church who heard us preach and teach this for six years, this Christian black man shows up during BLM week, and it's like, "Whoa, these are my people. There are other people like me in this world, and they kind of marginally did church, too, but now, we're doing it and so I've got something to offer them, but I've got a community now..." And I said to our church, I said, "This was a gift to us because we began to see the ministries to which we are called manifest before us." It was a glimpse of God's glory for us, so that we could be drawn into the work more fully... I mean, this is a remarkable gift to us.

Safe Space, Sanctuary Space

Jacquelyn Foster is the pastor of Compton Heights Christian Church (Disciples of Christ) in south St. Louis city. The church is located in a section of the city that has a significant amount of economic and racial diversity in very close proximity. The congregation is predominately white, and found itself in the midst of another set of protests when Vonderrit Myers was killed by an off-duty police officer on October 8 a few blocks away from their church. She reflects on the responses toward racial justice work their congregation did in the aftermath of Brown's and Myers' deaths.

Michael Brown was shot in August. In our denomination, Reconciliation Sunday is the end of September and early October. Reconciliation Ministries is the antiracism, pro-reconciling ministry of Christian Church (Disciples of Christ). And so all of that came together in a kind of an interesting way because a couple in our congregation were involved in a gathering for conversation that was on public television or public radio in which the "Race Card Project" was used. As they gathered, they had all been given cards with the word "race" on them and asked to respond in six words or less. And some of those responses then ended up being a part of this conversation. So they brought that idea back to us and said, "Okay, during our reconciliation focus in these weeks, let's do a version of the Race Card Project in worship each Sunday."

For three weeks in worship in late September/early October we had mission moments with cards that were in people's worship bulletins or handed out. The first week, the card said "race" and asked for people to respond briefly to what came to mind. The second week, the word was "reconciliation" and they were asked to respond to what came to mind. On the third week, it wasn't a response to a word but the question "What would you like to see us do now? How do we take action?" And so that was how we began the conversation within the congregation in the month after Michael Brown's death.

It was interesting that, on the night of October 8, our elders' circle was gathered, and the elders had, at that point, two weeks' worth of these cards and so they had the ones reflecting on race and reconciliation. The last one wasn't in yet. So the elder circle was gathered and it seemed like every elder was there that night, and they were reflecting on these cards. The chair of the elders handed out all these cards around the group, so you didn't have necessarily your own card. You didn't know who wrote which one. And we spent this evening talking about race and the pain of racial injustice, and when we came out of that meeting Vonderrit Myers had been killed five blocks down the street.

The irony to us was that we had been having this sometimes-tearful conversation about racism and about racial profiling and about police violence, and right in the middle of it this young man was shot and killed. I think the difficulty came when we found out that he had been shot by an off-duty police officer who was doing security for a nearby street. That hit home to us in a very direct way. This congregation is a mixed-raced congregation and houses Isaiah 58 Ministries, which is food pantry, health services and employment support ministry within the community. We have experienced, over time, the use of this security service to try to run black poor people away from our property. There have been a lot of complaints about us as kind of a nuisance, feeling that we draw black poor people to this area, which is kind of a funny thing. I mean that—you know, because that's who our neighbors are, except not on this street so much. So we had experienced some negative things with that security service and so it hit home in a way and, I think, drew us in. The next night, we ended up hosting an ecumenical prayer service here in our sanctuary, and that was with representation from churches and pastors all through the neighborhood. The alderman and I worked on pulling that together. So —that really stepped up the congregation's engagement once the shooting in our neighborhood happened.

Then we began going and taking part in holding vigil at the makeshift memorial where Vonderrit was killed, and I got on the schedule. MCU [Metropolitan Congregations United] was scheduling people at places at the police department in Ferguson and at the memorial here at that place. I would do Thursday nights at the memorial here and began engaging with Vonderrit Myers' parents and family and gathering there and having conversation with people and—and I think that that was transforming for me in a way because what I heard was people being afraid.

And I knew what it was to be afraid, but I think in the protest marches, everything was portrayed by the media so that it looked scary from the outside. But when you were in it, it wasn't. I remember, on the march from here to Saint Louis University the night that we were doing the "Occupy SLU" around the clock tower, I didn't know where we were going. Somebody knew where we were going, but I didn't know. My husband and I, we're just walking. And the conversations around us and the faith conversations around us, somebody was singing hymns back behind us, and it was this combination of mostly young people. We were pretty much old in that crowd, [laughs] but it was purposeful, and it was a gathering of thoughtful, for the most part, thoughtful visionary young people.

And I remember we got up onto the bridge, and the police are doing their thing over there, blocking not only the street but the sidewalk, and the leaders were very organized in keeping people on the sidewalk. Obey the law, keep people on the sidewalk. The police are doing their dance, they're beating the batons on the street, and this young black woman and man, right next to me, looked over at me, and she said, "Do you have anything to protect yourself from pepper spray?" And I said, "I don't know that I do." And she said, "Well, here, you've got a turtleneck. Is okay if I spray some vinegar water in here?" And I said, "Yes." And they were making sure that my husband and I were going to be okay. And I just saw this kind of caring that was really moving. So the police finally open the bridge back up. There was no pepper spray at that time, and we went on to the SLU campus, where I saw this amazing scene.

We're walking down past the dorms and the library is over here, and people are looking out the windows. And some of them are in their pajamas, and, pretty soon, they're coming out the doors and joining in. As the protestors came in, they were kind of beckoning for them to come out, and so we saw this coming together of college students and other protestors who were there. And we were standing there, and Vonderrit Myers' father had spoken, and there were some speeches and chants. And I remember an older black pastor coming over to another pastor, these two men next to me, and he said, "The kids have done it. We couldn't do it, but the kids have done it."

And I know that it wasn't the way they imagined because every once in a while, I would hear them say, "Language, language!" [laughs] They were wanting the kids to clean up the language — but as they were saying, "Language, language," they would also say, "But the kids have done it." And they hugged each other, and you know I can't know all of what they meant in that moment. I guess what I saw and what I read in it is the kids had stepped out there and said, "We are not going to live like this without voice anymore." The kids had pulled together an energy and a movement that was not stopping. The kids were getting the attention of the city. The kids were pulling together people who did not think they would be on the streets doing this.

I just saw hope there: hope for a different future; hope that black lives would matter; hope that the killing of young black people and particularly young black men would not just be accepted as the way it is. Hope—I guess, and when I think about it, I begin to lay my theological stuff on it. So here, when we gather as Christian Church (Disciples of Christ), when we have communion every Sunday and that's just a part of who we are, a phrase we use a lot is going out from this table to set the table in the streets. That image that we set the table in the streets and everybody is at that table, that's the kingdom of God. That's the reign of God. That's the culture of God. That's how I see that hope, I guess, but

I'm always careful. As a white person in this, it's good and fair and right that, because we're all in this together, that I have my hopes for it, but the most important thing is the hope of those who are black, and I always feel a little hesitant to lay my—I don't want to name somebody else's hope. But I have a hope.

When we were anticipating the Grand Jury decision about the indictment or non-indictment of Darren Wilson in the killing of Michael Brown, the congregation was asked if we would become a "safe space," and so we said yes, with understanding that, at that point, St. John's Episcopal on Arsenal would be the "sanctuary space" in this area. That would be a sanctuary for protestors, kind of safe place for them as the community planned for whatever would happen after that announcement. And we would be a safe space, which would be a place for anyone in the community to come to be together, to pray, to talk, and that we would be open for 24 hours, at least, after that announcement. We said yes to that and then we were contacted by Waltrina Middleton, who is the national youth coordinator for the United Church of Christ. She was working with an MCU group, and they were looking for space where they could train young people for nonviolent protests and asked if we had such space, and we said yes. We kept going back and forth to the trustees or to the elders, saying, "Well, we have this need…then there's this need," and then there was need for a place for people to cook for the protest. And they weren't able to find a space in Ferguson that would have that and so we said sure.

We had this very interesting group of things going on when we opened up for this safe space. So it kind of turned into safe space and sanctuary space because the protestors or groups of protestors were coming in for training before they would go out on the streets. The hope was that, as young protestors came into town or as school groups came—for instance, we had a group from Wash U. and a group from SLU of kids who came, and they came in for training, so that they could learn how to go out on the street with purpose and hopefully not get caught up in groups that were not going out with as much purpose or a positive purpose. People came in to be trained to be legal observers. And so, as the protest was going on, as the streets out here were full of protestors, they would come in and out of the building, and then, as, unfortunately, the tear-gassing was happening down the street and some couldn't get to St. John's, and they came back up here.

We really ended up being a broader kind of space... There were hundreds. It was a constant flow with lots of church members just staffing the space, just here to be welcoming. There was music and candlelight going on in the sanctuary. There was a room with the television on, so that people who wanted to stay connected to the news could. There was a room with art opportunities, so that people could express themselves just by coloring or drawing. There were coffee and tea and soup and just places for people to be.

I walked through the sanctuary at one time and there was a young woman who had come. She was a part of the group training for protest, and she had come up, and she was just sitting in the sanctuary praying. And she was crying, and I could tell she was really upset. And I stopped to talk to her for a minute, and she said, "I lost my church tonight." And she had just this deep sense that her church community could not see, could not be supportive of her as she protested. And I was downstairs at another moment, and one of the groups asked if I would pray before they went out, and I talked a minute about that they were a very diverse group. I didn't know their religious backgrounds or whatever, if any, but they just wanted that blessing. There were protestors in here who—coming up to us and wanting to give us money. And we said, "We don't want any money"—and there were a couple that said, "No, we want to give." There were protestors who asked me, "Why have you done this? Why are your doors open to us?" They wanted to support the church. I told them we did this because God loves them and God wants a just world and that we're called to do this. And they just thanked us and went on their way. So I think that it made a difference that the church—this church, at least, said, "We are with you."

Clock tower occupation on the St. Louis
University campus. *(Photo by David Carson/
St. Louis Post-Dispatch/Polaris)*

St. John's United Church of Christ hosts #blacklivesmatter Freedom Riders.
(Photo by Darnell L. Moore)

CHAPTER 8

There Is a Ferguson Near You

*"Earth is so thick with divine possibility that it is a wonder we
can walk anywhere without cracking our shins on altars."*

Barbara Brown Taylor

In her book *An Altar in the World,* Barbara Brown Taylor invites the reader to see and act upon everyday opportunities to meet up with the Divine. This is a call to a particular kind of awakening that beckons us to see the Godlike opportunities in our daily experiences. Experiencing God is not relegated to ecstatic experiences, nor can we force their occurrence. Instead, we become more conscious of "divine possibility" in our world—and especially in those places that yearn for a different, more thriving existence.

"Divine possibility" has motivated many of the works of the clergy and been revealed by the actions of young activists in this movement for racial justice. Traci Blackmon described her "God moments" in the early days of her work after Michael Brown was killed. These were opportunities that she believed embodied God's ethos of care and compassion for the suffering. David Gerth's witness of the young activists' tenacious diligence and focus during the protest in front of the Ferguson police station while the clergy kneeled on the sidewalk was recognized as a Godlike moment. Gerth's perspective about this movement was transformed in that moment, when he saw the young activists embodying a spirit of power that he recognized as the spirit of God. These and other occurrences enable us to perceive and ponder how God may be at work in the movement for racial justice, and consider how we may be called, wherever we may be.

The racial injustices revealed in the aftermath of Michael Brown's death are not unique to Ferguson, St. Louis, or even Missouri. The killing of Michael Brown was not an isolated incident, and it happened within weeks of several other high profile police killings of black men around the country. In New York, Eric Garner, 43, was unarmed and died from asphyxiation after being stopped by police for allegedly selling loose cigarettes. Ezell Ford, 25, who was unarmed and had a history of mental illness, was stopped for an unknown reason by police while walking down a Los Angeles street and shot to death. John Crawford, 22, was looking at merchandise while holding a BB/pellet gun in an Ohio Wal-Mart store when a police officer shot and killed him. Tamir Rice, 12, was killed by a Cleveland police officer while holding a toy gun on a playground. None of the police officers were held liable for these deaths, and it is in this broader context that the corresponding actions related to Michael Brown took place.

While this movement for racial justice has been sparked by the police killing of an unarmed young black man, broader instances of racial injustice that are evidenced in income, education, health, and incarceration disparities—to name a few—have re-entered the public discourse to demand needed attention. Realizing the ways in which these issues intersect with each other, it is reasonable and expected they would emerge. Out of their emergence comes a realization that this is not just a Ferguson issue, but that these issues are present around the St. Louis region and the United States.

It Is in Our Backyard

Chesterfield, Missouri, is an affluent western suburb of St. Louis. Shortly after Michael Brown was killed, a Unitarian Universalist congregation in Chesterfield took action in particular ways that brought attention to the issue of racial injustice in St. Louis. Krista Taves, the congregational minister at Emerson Unitarian Universalist Chapel, reflects on the implications of their work.

Our congregation is located in West St. Louis County, one of the most affluent areas of our region. Our members are predominantly white middle class, university educated, and many of them are from other parts of the country because this is a transitory area. Most of them are not native St. Louisans.

Last year, we did yearlong, antiracism, multiculturalism training for the congregation called "Building the World We Dream About," which is produced by the Unitarian Universalist Association. I encouraged the congregation to do this work for many reasons. We were doing service work with schools in the poorest areas of our city [St. Louis], most of which had predominantly black students, and we built a relationship with the Kensington Community in St. Louis. We had to do this internal work to understand the context in which we were trying to serve.

The program was completed in May [2014] and we made plans to have four individuals give testimonies in an August service. The week before that service, Michael Brown was killed. We had to respond. I worked with those [four] individuals to tailor the worship service to include a response to the shooting and what was happening in the streets. The first two testimonies were what had been planned. The second two testimonies were from people who wanted to respond directly to what they were seeing, who were already preparing to go into the streets. They talked about police brutality and racial profiling, about the killing of unarmed black men by white police officers, about the school-to-prison pipeline. And to the surprise of many, including me, people walked out. They walked out of the service because they felt that it was bashing the police and that their church was taking sides. That's how it started for us in this white, predominantly middle class congregation in far West County.

Responding to the call for action became a defining issue for our social justice team, which began to meet on a weekly basis. How were we going to respond? There weren't a lot of ideas at the beginning. Everybody wanted to do something, but nobody knew what to do. These are some of the responses that took place in the larger congregation. Many people in our church said, "Oh, my goodness. I used to live in Ferguson. This was my hometown. This was my community." They expressed deep concern for the community and pain at the divisions and the conflict. Only one person ever said why their family no longer lived there. Only one member of our church said, "The reason I'm going to the vigils is because my grandparents left Ferguson because they didn't want to live around blacks. That's why I'm standing vigil because I'm complicit in this." Everybody else mentioned their family's move but not the reasons for it. I found that a really interesting disconnect.

Then there were those who had difficulty with the term "black lives matter." They asked, "Why don't all lives matter? Why are you picking sides? Unitarian Universalism affirms the inherent worth and dignity of every person. By saying 'black lives matter,' you are silencing everybody else who is a person of color who's not black, and you're also discriminating." Then there were those who said, "I'm totally in support of equality. I know that there is racism in our city. I know that there is marginalization and poverty, and that it's connected to racial violence, but they chose the wrong victim in Michael Brown. He was a thug because he smoked up. He robbed a convenience store, and they have put their eggs in a bad basket."

There was also some expressed discomfort with the choice of using civil disobedience, shutting down highways and blocking off intersections. There was a real, visceral reaction to black anger or anyone who chose to share in that anger. In the reactions, you could see them connecting anger with violence— that to express anger was violent. For instance, after the non-indictment of Darren Wilson…I expressed anger at the decision, and I received considerable criticism from one person who said it was inappropriate for me to express anger, that she didn't want anger from her minister. She wanted peace from her minister. By expressing anger I wasn't supporting peace. There has been implicit and explicit pressure on me and on other members of the congregation to temper the message, to make it palatable to that white, middle class sensibility, as if to say, "Please don't make me uncomfortable. Let me be comfortable again."

Some said, "I'm concerned that you're going to be pushing guests away. You're preaching about this too much." I understood this to mean, "You're going to be pushing white guests away." I did not stop preaching. And I felt it was my moral responsibility not to stop talking. I did not want to give in to the pressure, to go back to the status quo. I see that a lot in the white community out here. I call it "the great white silence of West County." I felt it was my responsibility not to be silent, or I would be complicit with the continued violence being done to black communities in our city.

I guess I shouldn't have been surprised at the pushback, but I was disappointed. How could we live in this environment and not be changed by the environment in which we live? Me included? White privilege includes huge blinders about race and the expectation to be able to keep those blinders to stay comfortable. This experience really holds up for me that white privilege is ignorance. White privilege is assuming one has the norm on meaning and understanding and the appropriate display of emotion. Experiencing the power of this privilege has been sobering. Despite the resistance, the emerging situation in Ferguson and on the streets of our city did motivate and coalesce and focus our social justice team, and they actually haven't blinked.

We began joining the Eliot Unitarian Chapel vigil in Kirkwood. Eliot provided a venue, and members of our church who wanted to do something, anything, attended. Ten to twelve members of our church took part. Then, on the Ferguson October weekend, I invited two members of our church to give testimonials. One is a young woman, a teenager, Cambodian, adopted by a white single mother living in Chesterfield. This young woman has gone through hell being a person of color in Chesterfield. I asked if she would tell the story of what she has experienced here. Could she help the congregation bring the message home? She called her testimony "The County Brownie, Death by 1,000 Cuts." Her mother also gave a testimonial called "White Soccer Mom." She talked about her feelings of helplessness and rage at not being able to protect her daughter. The tears in that service were unbelievable. That's what brought it home. The relationship they had with that family brought it home. I asked the congregation, "What is our response to this? Because this is here. What's happening in Ferguson is here. It is in our backyard. It is in our homes. It is in our schools. It is on our streets. It is in our malls. It's at Walgreens where this girl gets asked to leave her purse every time she goes shopping. How are we going to stand together as a community?"

Moms on the Move

There is something about "bringing it home" that helps to connect people with a reality they perceive to be radically different from their own. One of the ways this happened in the aftermath of Michael Brown's death was through hearing the stories of black mothers of raising sons in today's world. Christi Griffin, the executive director of The Ethics Project in St. Louis, is a mother and grandmother of black men. She believed that more white mothers needed to hear black mothers' experiences of what it is like to raise sons in a society that too often assumes them to be a threat. Dr. Griffin organized a dozen or so black mothers of sons to gather before a predominately white audience and share five-minute testimonials about their experiences. She called this event Mother 2 Mother.

The first event was held before a crowd of about 250 people at the Missouri History Museum in St. Louis. Word about this event spread, and it became a little movement unto itself, spreading the often-unheard perspectives of black mothers. Demand increased and five additional events took place around the St. Louis region. The hope for these events was to create a kind of awareness about young black men through the perspectives of their mothers that was not steeped in stereotypes, but in the reality of their lived experiences. The hope was for the mothers in the audience to relate to the mothers onstage *as mothers,* and see young black men through the lens *of a mother,* and be inspired to work to make our world a safer place for all of our children.

One of the other calls for mothers to come together was during the Mother's March on October 18. "Three Pastors and a Professor" organized this march: Karen Anderson, Traci Blackmon, Rebecca Ragland, and myself. Its purpose was to bring mothers together to call for justice on behalf of Michael Brown, and call for an end to all violence in our city.

Our mantra was "praying with our feet until there is no more blood in our streets," and we rallied in front of and marched around the block of the St. Louis County. Hundreds of mothers participated in this multi-racial event, and we collectively lamented the loss of lives to violence, and called for an end to all killings of our children at the hands of police, people claiming "stand your ground" justifications, or peers.

Rebecca Ragland was serving as pastor of the Episcopal Church of the Holy Communion in University City, Missouri in late 2014. She describes her entrance into this movement and the way her congregation "prayed with their feet" in their town:

The first time I heard about Michael Brown's death was Sunday morning during worship. At the 8:00 service, one of our members untraditionally — we usually don't have people speak during the announcements about prayer concerns—stood up and said that there had been a shooting and that there was a lot of concern about the shooting and that he wanted us to pray about it, and so we prayed about it.

My first response was to find out what the other clergy were doing because I didn't see Ferguson as my zone. I didn't know where Ferguson was per se. I guess we all live in zones, and it was outside of my zone. So I was waiting to look for leadership that I trust, and by Wednesday night it was appalling watching what was unfolding on television. On Thursday morning, Traci Blackmon sent out the text message to say clergy were gathering at her church, and I was there.

That was the first point at which I really started, and then there was no stopping in terms of being involved. The march that afternoon, I contacted my congregation. We were there, and from then on, I was at West Florissant during the day and into the night. I was in somewhat of a unique situation in that I was about six months into an interim at the church in which I had been serving for about eight years in different capacities. I started there in seminary, and I've been there all the way through. So we have a long relationship, and I know, historically, that this church, it's a diverse community. It's a community that has not dodged issues of race and issues of power, and so it was prepared, in some respects, psychologically, for this trauma.

And so there was a pretty decent level of participation given the number of people who are older in the congregation. There was a pretty good level of participation in that early event on the Thursday afternoon after Mike Brown's death. We had about 14 people from the congregation who marched. And so that was important for us to really show our solidarity. About 10 days after that, we had a prayer vigil at the church, and we marched from the church with our youth in leadership to the University City High School, which is not far from us. And we had a prayer and liturgy in front of the high school. It was sort of a way of showing our solidarity both with the youth and also identifying that this isn't just an issue that is related to Ferguson but is, in fact, a nationwide issue.

Mommy, Why Are They Doing This?

DeMarco Davidson is a seminary student and the president of the consistory for St. John's UCC in St. Louis. He reflects on his congregation's immediate response and describes one of the ways he helped create public awareness of the movement:

I was actually heading to a family event. My dad and I were driving down Chambers Road when we got sidelined by several cop cars that were not from area. So my dad and I, we were like, "Uh-oh," with all the cops coming from different municipalities. When that happens, it usually means a cop has been wounded, so we wanted to pray for that family. After we got to our family event, some of my friends started calling my phone. The sun was still up, and my friend was like, "Man, did you hear what happened?" Well, then I looked on Facebook and I saw actual pictures of Mike Brown laying in the street....and then I also saw a picture with the trail of blood coming from his body, and it just broke my heart.

When I went home, I kept listening to what was going on on the radio, because they preempted programming on the radio. So they actually stopped playing the normal corporate playlist, and they actually were playing somewhat uplifting, empowering songs. Like the normal hip-hop station that unfortunately plays a lot of the normal popular/negative music. They actually stopped. So instead of playing killing type songs, they were playing Public Enemy's "Fight the Power." They played the song "Self Destruction." "We All in the Same Gang." Like they literally played all of Queen Latifah's "U-N-I-T-Y." They started playing those songs on August 9. So August 10, when I woke up they were still having certain conversations, but they already started playing the same corporate playlist of songs.

So I went to church where Rev. Starsky Wilson is the pastor, and it was very tough. He wanted to focus on the long-term movement aspect of keeping things upfront, so he asked everybody who was involved with youth—teachers, community leaders, and leaders of the church—to come up, get a book, and we had to all read it and actually write a two-page reflection on it. And naturally, me being the president of the consistory, basically being one of the elders and trustees and also a mentor, somebody who worked in the community, I had to get a book. I was happy to, and I was glad that Starsky already had somewhat of a plan of action, as well as something to give us to refocus our energy, because a lot of people were feeling a huge amount of pain, but now we also have a vision.

On August 14, it was like three or four in the morning. I was on the phone with my friend. We couldn't sleep. We couldn't sleep like the first two weeks. One thing that I took from when things happened with Trayvon Martin, people—some people—like had pictures of them in hoodies or blacked out their Facebook page, things like that. But you don't really see Trayvon Martin's face that much anymore, and one thing I wanted was, I wanted Mike Brown's face to continue to be seen all the time. I don't want us to forget his face. So I was like, "Man, we should make a bunch of Mike Brown masks and just go places and just stand there."

Soon we were together at his place cutting out masks of Mike Brown, and we ordered over 200 American fla gs. We had about 200 masks. We ended up getting a group of about 30, 40 people together. We went out to one of the Cardinals baseball games. So this was the—to my understanding—this was the first [action] that was outside of Ferguson. There were some people who actually did like outline, like pseudo chalk outlines of people, but it was like somebody did it and they were gone. We actually got together and met in Kiener Plaza. We handed everybody a mask and directions on what to do. Then we went to the Cardinals game. When they started playing the National Anthem we all put on a mask. And we didn't just keep it at Mike Brown. We also had Trayvon Martin, even a young Eric Garner mask, even a John Crawford, and I do believe a couple of others.

But we all put on the masks, laid down on the ground where people were going into the Cardinals game so they would have to step over us and walk over us, and we held American flags up as if we were almost like at a cemetery site. The goal was we wanted people to know that these are American citizens that are being murdered, being killed, and these are young people. We wanted people to see their faces and associate the American flag with this new, not necessarily new but this repackaged, form of terrorism that people are experiencing.

I think that was probably the most scary moment of my life just because I'm on the ground, and I never knew the National Anthem was so long. When the National Anthem was over, we all got up and said, "Hands up, don't shoot," 10 times, and we walked off. As we were walking away, some of the African Americans who were working at the ballpark said, "Can I please have one of those masks?" We were like, "Sure. That's no problem." Then we started to debrief. A lot of people immediately felt the tension and I think that's when we realized what we were up against. We heard several comments. One of the comments was, "I wish I had a gun right now. I'd kill them all. What are they doing out here? Oh, this is so stupid. Oh, my god. They're doing it out here now." And this was before people got into it at the baseball stadium and all of that, and this was before people got into it at the football stadium and all that.

But one of the greatest things that I personally heard—and I don't know if it actually will result in anything different or not—but I heard a little white boy have to ask his white mother, "Mommy, why are they doing this?" So the fact that she now has to have that conversation is important. That's why we're doing this, and I pray and I hope that she takes that as an education moment instead of a fill it with hate moment because she could easily turn it around. She could manipulate it. She could just say, "Oh, they're doing it because some young thug was killed," or something. I mean she could say because they're protecting a criminal. She could come up with anything, but I hope it's positive. Now this conversation is in their home. It is not just in our homes anymore.

I remember the first time I had to have that conversation with my mom. I was actually 18, and I was driving through Calverton Park. It's only like four streets big. I got pulled over one night after leaving a fundraising activity for a leadership development program that I was president of, and I'm already planning on going to college anyway. So like, I'm an excellent student, and I had my cousin with me who already had a football scholarship going to college.

But we were seniors in high school. We got pulled over. We had to sit on the curb. They ransacked my car and all that, and they said, "Oh, your car looked like somebody's car," and all that. Well, we were well-mannered and all that, but this is ridiculous. We already knew we were innocent, but I was infuriated at how they searched us and treated us like we had committed a crime or something. I went home mad, went home infuriated, and talked to my mom, and my mom said, "Well, baby. That's just the way it is." And I was like, "No. That's not the way it is," and I almost cursed at my momma for the first time. Like I almost cursed at her because I was so upset that she felt that this is an okay thing to experience or to deal with. I was 18. So Mike Brown is personal to me for multiple reasons.

So on that Sunday, Reverend Starsky gave an outstanding sermon. It was a tough sermon where he even asked, what if Mike Brown was our Jesus Christ? What if Mike Brown was the thing that pushed us to the point of doing God's true work that's needed to be done? And I started thinking I need to start studying and learning what has been done before, what has been done in the past. I ended up doing research on Mamie Till, Emmett Till's mother. I connected Mike Brown and Emmett Till simply because it was a public display of destruction of a young man, of a kid, of a child.

That to me was one of the things that sparked the movement in the '50s and '60s with Emmett Till's death because his mother decided to have an open casket funeral, and that image was in black publications like *Jet* magazine. They felt that pain and expressed that destruction. So Martin King rose from that, even Malcolm X and other movements, things like that. This year, in 2015, will be the 60th anniversary of Emmett Till's death. I recently saw a clip on YouTube that had a 30th anniversary in 1985 with Mamie Till, and she was saying the same exact things that Leslie McSpadden was saying, same exact things. She was saying how she was hurt. It was painful. She never thought this would happen to her child. She knew things like this happened, she just never thought it would happen to her. She also mentioned how the people who murdered her son said that they felt justified for doing it. Very similar to what we heard after Mike Brown was killed. So when I heard that, I was like, wait a minute, there's something else going on here because, apparently, there's some type of fear of black boys that has to be addressed.

Krista Taves continues her description of Emerson U.U. Chapel's response to the killing of Michael Brown. In this section, she reflects on the public actions they took in an attempt to "awaken" their local community to the economic and social injustices that disproportionately affect black people.

At the next social justice meeting, we decided to schedule vigils to begin the first Saturday of November. We're in the heart of white flight [in Chesterfield]. We have the largest mall in the [metropolitan area]; the largest symbol of consumerism is in our backyard. We chose to hold vigil outside the Chesterfield Commons every Saturday from 11:30 [a.m.] to 12:30 [p.m.], and that is what we have been doing since November, with no plans to discontinue. It has been a very eye-opening experience for many of our members. We have a core of about five people who go just about every week. We have members of Eliot Chapel in Kirkwood who join us regularly, including their lead minister, and also others who are not Unitarian Universalist. Unitarian Universalists from out of town have come to stand with us, including a colleague. We stand at the intersection of Boone's Crossing and Airport Chesterfield Road every Saturday for an hour. We hold our signs: "black lives matter," "white silence is violence," "liberty and justice for all." We hold our "standing on the love" banner. "Standing on the Side of Love" is our "brand" for social justice work. Whenever you see the big yellow signs saying, "Standing on the Side of Love," that's Unitarian Universalists. We are in the yellow T-shirts, sweatshirts, hats, and stoles.

After the vigil, we meet up at a local coffee shop and process what we've experienced and discuss next steps. Our vigil thus contains witnessing, processing, caring for each other, community building and planning, and information sharing. The original intent of the vigil, which still remains true, is to witness to the predominantly white population of Chesterfield that this issue is alive, that there are white people who stand with people of color and that we have work to do at home.

The other part of the witness, which was not our explicit plan but...has happened, is to witness to blacks that there are whites in the county who support them. Our vigil is just down from a bus stop. And who rides the buses? It's the people who work in Chesterfield, many of whom are black and Hispanic. We know that they've been on that bus for two hours to get to their minimum wage jobs in the Chesterfield Commons. They're getting off the bus in a city that provides them no bus shelters and no sidewalks, and they're walking right by us. As the bus pulls away, you can see people watching us as they go by. This has been an important ministry.

Then there are others, who come to shop. We get the Black Power symbol. We get honking and thank yous. The most positive response we get is from blacks. It's very clear. From whites the response is mixed. Some people honk at us and give us the thumbs up. Mostly there is silence. People try not to look at us. We do get some belligerent people every week. We get sworn at. We get the finger shot at us. We get the "all lives matter." We get "support the police." It was strongest and most aggressive the weeks before the Grand Jury reveal. Tensions were very high. That has tapered off. Now we just get a lot of shooting the finger and swearing.

As this vigil continues, we know it's not going to last forever. Eventually our vigil will stop. Where do we go next? We've had some ideas, such as working with the Chesterfield Police Department to address their practices. We know that racial profiling is a problem here.

The other is to work with the St. Louis Public Transportation about having bus shelters, having sidewalks, having benches, just these basic things, so that the people who come out to work in Chesterfield actually have shelter and a place to sit while they're waiting for the bus and a safe way to walk to work. Right now they're walking alongside Chesterfield Airport Road. They're walking right next to the traffic.

The other issue is revenue sharing... The whole region shops at the Chesterfield Commons ... Taxpayer dollars built the levees that created Chesterfield Valley... All that money is staying in Chesterfield, a community that is already one of the wealthiest in the region. How can we be part of that conversation? How can we stand for a different way of being in our region?

Mother's March in Clayton on October 18, 2014. *(Photo by Stephanie Scott-Huffman)*

"Mother 2 Mother" event at Temple Emanuel on January 26, 2015. *(Photo by Philip Deitch)*

Emerson Chapel Unitarians protesting in Chesterfield Valley. *(Photo by Jake Lyonfields)*

Protesters don masks to remind everyone of the individuals killed. *(Photo by Sir Erwin J. Williams)*

CHAPTER 9

Standing on the Side of Love

"Without justice there can be no love."

bell hooks

The protest journey toward racial justice took a decidedly different turn on October 4 to Powell Hall, home of the St. Louis Symphony Orchestra. Just before the start of Act II of Brahms' *A German Requiem*, a few audience members stood up and began singing the lines below to the tune of Florence Reece's protest song "Which Side Are You On?" As more people stood and sang:

> *Which side are you on, friend?*
> *Which side are you on?*
> *Justice for Mike Brown is*
> *Justice for us all!*

It became clearer this was an organized protest effort. The musicians sat still in their seats and guest conductor Markus Stenz stood still as a statue at his post as the protestors sang and draped four banners over the balcony that read "Requiem for Mike Brown (1996–2014)," "Racism Lives Here" with an arrow pointing toward an arch, "Rise up and join the movement," and a picture of Brown with "Mike Brown 1996–2014." At the end of the two-minute song, dozens of protestors walked out while chanting "black lives matter" as red paper hearts that read "Requiem for Mike Brown" cascaded over the balcony.

"Which side are you on?" is a common question that has been posed or implied since Michael Brown was killed. What is often intended is to force a choice between the side of the police or the protestors. For many of the clergy that engaged in this movement, their choice was not framed as being *for* the protestors and *against* the police. Instead, their choice was often framed as standing on the side of love, and, for them, "love" meant doing the work of God, which is the work of justice. For many, to stand with the protestors meant standing firm on what they believed was consistent with the tenets of their faith. It did not mean that they are fundamentally "against" the police.

That clergy stood in the gap of this perceived chasm between protestors and police was evidenced most clearly after two police officers were shot on March 12, 2015, shortly after Ferguson Police Chief Tom Jackson announced his resignation. This action was uncharacteristic of the protestors who had gathered regularly in front of the Ferguson police station since Brown's death, and many were skeptical that a person connected with the movement for racial justice committed this crime. The person later arrested for shooting the police officers had no known affiliation with the regular protestors or the any facets of the movement.

The day after the officers were shot, several clergy assembled in Ferguson to publically renounce these shootings and pray for the officers. Traci Blackmon gave the opening reflection and purpose of the gathering:

We are gathered here tonight. It occurred to me today, as we were preparing for this evening, that, over 200 days ago, we gathered on the parking lot of the Ferguson Police Department on August 10 to center ourselves in prayer, to anchor ourselves in the hope that we know that is real. Over 200 days ago, many of us met for the first time, gathered there, all drawn there with a call for justice, and 200 days later, we're still standing. And we're still here, and we've endured lots of trauma and lots of pain and lots of moments of loneliness during these 200 days.

There have been tense times and narrow times and angry times and hurting times and times when we couldn't do anything but cry during these 200 days. We've lost more lives and more lives over these 200 days, and we're still standing. So having come through all of that, talking just one to one over this last 24 hours, we recognize that what happened at the police station last night has not happened in those 200 days; that in our deepest of despair, in our hardest of moments, in our most angry times, we have not had what occurred last night. And so I am convinced, as I know many of you are convinced, that whatever was the cause, whoever was the culprit last night, that they did not come from this community that's been standing for 200 days.

And so we've come tonight to center ourselves one more time, to declare that this ground is indeed holy one more time and to declare that we will not be derailed in the pursuit of justice by anybody or anything that wants to get in our way. We come because we, as humans, are all connected, and we have not lost touch with our humanity. We come to grieve the wounding of law enforcement officers last night. We come to lament the death of a six-year-old boy...yesterday. We come to lament the death of those who will not go home ever again. We come to give God thanks that the officers who were injured last night are now at their homes. We come to give thanks that police officers were those who carried that little six-year-old boy in hope that they could make it to a hospital before he died. We come to remember that we are all connected, and until we recognize the humanity in one another, we cannot heal. So we refuse to stop. We refuse to let the enemy win this battle.

Over 200 days later, we're still standing, and we have not forgotten on that which we stand: a solid rock. We will not be moved. We will not give up and so we've come together this night to use the most powerful weapon we have and that is that of prayer—recognizing that, even as we pray in this space, there are those who are in Hazelwood praying for four lives lost in Hazelwood Central, recognizing that, as we pray in this place, there's a family in...north St. Louis planning a funeral for a child who will never see first grade, recognizing in this place that, when we have done all that we can, we must continue to stand.

If You're Not Part of the Solution, You're Part of the Problem

Susan Talve, the rabbi at Central Reformed Congregation in the Central West End neighborhood of St. Louis, describes the challenges some clergy are confronted with in their congregations and how she understands this facet of her work as integral to her faith tradition and identity.

Across the board, clergy—white and black—are often faced with difficulty in their congregations. Congregants say, "I don't want to hear about Ferguson anymore. If you're going to preach on that, I'm not coming." People have left. I mean, there's a real problem. It's happening to some rabbis in the county. They're being punished for their participation—even people who have done very little. It's like people feel so threatened by this. We have to get to the bottom of that, for sure. I have a lot of credibility because I helped build the congregation. But, even here—I wrote a piece called "Why I Stand with the Protestors," and I sent it out snail mail to my congregation. I wanted it to feel personal. I wanted it to feel like I was writing them a letter. And most people said to me, "Why did you feel like you had to write that letter? You think we don't support you?"

But I think that it's complicated for people because I show up at a lot of things. I'm there when somebody dies. I'm there when somebody's born. So I don't think people can say I'm not doing my work or, "She's always in Ferguson." But, you know, this is a line in the sand for me. There've been two other times in my career there's been a line in the sand. One was the women priests. I had to do that. I put it to my board. I said, "You get to decide this, but you have to also know it's a line in the sand for me. I'm not sure I can stay if we don't do this." I went, "Oh, I can't believe I said that," but I said it, and then, of course, it was unanimous. But we did have people leave over that, and it hasn't come to that here.

[The other line in the sand was] 12 years ago, a woman named Yavilah McCoy. She's an Orthodox Jew of color, third generation Orthodox Jew of color. And she led us through—12 years ago—a dismantling racism process for the whole congregation. That's why we're integrated today. I mean, it's a direct result of everybody reading a book. The whole board had to do work. Every circle in the community had to talk about it. All the teachers got training. We went on a retreat, and we did really hard work. I mean, I cried a lot because this congregation, a lot of people here marched in Selma. So there are a lot of Civil Rights heroes in this congregation. But you can't just say, "Oh, I'm good. I marched in Selma."

Part of the problem was we thought we knew, but people of color kept coming and then leaving and coming and leaving. We knew we were doing something wrong. So Yavilah came and she put us through this really deep kind of internal work, and, today, we're integrated. We are integrated. It took changing the liturgy. It took changing some of the music. It took changing the way we look. It took changing the artwork we have around. I mean, everything I have is Jews of color, everywhere.

So if I'm doing that and making this a safe place for Jews of color and I'm not out there fighting for them to be treated equally on the street, what am I doing? So it's a line in the sand for me, and if somebody says to me, "You can't do both," then I can't do this anymore. But they haven't done that, and I don't think they're going to do that because I think a lot of us share these values. People whisper to me all the time, "Thank you for what you're doing out there, Rabbi. Thank you for what you're doing." They whisper, "You know why? Because somebody has framed this as the people against the police. That's why, and it's not the people against the police." But the framing of this by [news media] and by people who have a lot to lose if we win, right, they have framed this about the people against the police. We have police officers who keep us safe during the holidays because there's a lot of anti-Semitism, and if it wasn't for our police officers, we couldn't be here. They keep us safe. We love them. Yet there is a lot that needs to change within the system.

Talve goes on to reflect on her early days of activism, and the correlations she sees with the Millennials and their movement for racial justice.

I think about this a lot in relation to my generation. I'm in my 60s, which meant I grew up in the '60s, and I was very influenced by the feminist movement, the anti-Vietnam War movement, and the Civil Rights Movement. My hero was Angela Davis. I tried to get her to come to my high school. I wrote her a letter. She said she'd come and then she got busy so she sent two Black Panthers that were amazing, and they gave a great story. This was a little suburb outside of New York City, which primarily was white at the time, and very few Jews, too. And so I thought it was the right thing to do. There we were. I think it was 1968, and I was a junior or senior in high school, and I arranged it. What I'm remembering is there was one subversive teacher who helped me, but he kind of stayed in the background. So the Black Panthers came. They gave a great talk, and I got suspended from school is what I remember from that. It wasn't just me. There were a couple of people on the student council, but those were very formative years for us.

Those were very important years for us. We really believed that we could change the world, and we were young enough to believe that we ended the war in Vietnam. I mean, I know now that we didn't. And then what happened was the Baby Boomers kind of went into "hibernation," as I call it. I think that many of us got into professions, and we said, "Oh, we're going to change the system from the inside." That was our way of saying, "Okay. We've got to give to our kids what our parents gave to us."

But what happened was the world really changed and so we empowered our children, who are the Millennials today, to believe that they could do anything, that they could change the world, too, because we believed we could. And, of course, if we could, they could. And so we filled them with all of these tools. We gave them, I think, the tools for thinking things through and to be empowered and to expect the world to be right and moral and responsive to them. And then the economy changed. A lot of things changed. The Echo Boom [or Millennial Generation] was as big as the Baby Boom, but the world didn't have as much room. So they have had a harder time of it.

And so I think what happened, at least to our beautiful Millennials here across the country and the world, is they saw Mike Brown's body laying in the street for four and a half hours on a hot St. Louis day. And they got that it could have been any one of them—especially the kids of color, and it wasn't okay.

And for the kids who weren't of color that got involved, they said, "That could be my friend. That's not right." Enough of them had friends who were black and brown that they got it. I think it touched them in a very deep way and I think it broke open their hearts, and they said "no more" because—you know what?—we set them up. We set them up to believe that they mattered more than that, and that's what they're telling us: black lives matter.

Many clergy have expressed this sentiment: that it was the young people whose sense of self-worth propelled them to stand up and fight to be seen as human, and have their dignity affirmed. Talve goes on to talk about the work as being inextricably linked to her faith tradition.

For the Jewish community, it's in every prayer. It's in every holiday. It's in every teaching in the Torah that, until all people are free, not one of us is free, that we cannot stand idly by. Again, I'm thinking about those young people. If I don't walk the walk, I don't get to talk the talk because they're going to call me on it. I've been talking to them about "tikkun olam," repairing the world, for a long time. If they don't see me out there, what are they going to think? "She's a big talker, but she doesn't mean it." I think I have to be accountable to my community. I don't know if I could sleep at night if I didn't feel like I was doing something. This is an epidemic. There's something terrible happening. It's not my son getting profiled. I know that. It's not my son. When I say, "Hands up, don't shoot," they're not going to shoot me. I know that. But I think, "If I am not acutely aware of my privilege, as a white person, I am forgetting everything that ever happened to my people—because we have been profiled and we have been provoked and we have been 'other' so many times in history that, for the honor and the sake of my ancestors, who were profiled and provoked and killed just because of who they were, I recognize this as a hate crime. I recognize this, and I can't be part of it."

We say, "If you're not part of the solution, you're part of the problem, and that by complacently…sitting by, you're as guilty as anybody else." And that's the whole Torah. It's about leveling the playing field. It's about understanding systems of oppression and seeing how they set people up to fail. When you have a system where, because...poverty and racism together don't allow some people to escape, and some kids start school with 30,000 words less than somebody else's kid who had a little more, you can't say, "Well, everybody's got public education," and that should level the playing field. I actually had a really smart, caring white Jewish guy say to me the other day, "I don't get it. I grew up poor. I had a lot of challenges growing up, and look at me today." I said, "Are you kidding me?" I know, as Jews, we feel "other" in America and we feel that we have strikes against us, but until we understand—at least the white Jews—begin to understand that we have become part of white America, we are not going to make the sacrifices that are necessary to be an important part of this movement. So that's, I feel like, part of my work, too, and I'm not exactly sure how to do that other than to model it, to be there.

So for people of faith across the country and maybe even across the world, what are the things that you can do that will spark that excitement and that hope that you really can make a difference in your community? And then, as we continue to find our Fergusons across the nation, [what can we do to make sure] that we will really make a difference for everyone, because we keep saying we've taken a moment and we're desperately trying to build a movement. So what people do—not just here but out there—is really important, and it could be as simple as finding your Ferguson. If you're in a community, get to know your police officers and make sure they know your children and your neighbor's children. Get to know them. Make sure, if there are kids of color in your community, that there are programs that help them get to know the police and the police to get to know them by name, so that nobody makes judgments that aren't true and there are no mistaken identities.

If you're in a primarily white community, do your work. Understand your privilege. Dismantle your own racism and figure out a way to use your privilege for good—not to hide, not to build more walls, but use your privilege to build bridges. Take the walls down. Find out what the profiling laws are in your community and what the disparities are. See if you have communities around you that are victims of the school-to-prison pipelines that are feeding the prison industrial complex through mass incarceration.

These are things you can find out. You can Google these things. Everybody can know these things. Reach across the color divide. Make friends. Real friends. Nothing's going to change in America if we stay as segregated as we are, and if you have schools that are integrated by deseg programs, don't think that that's the answer. Look at how those kids are getting to know each other. Look at how they are relating to each other, and how they're treated by staff. Make sure that, in your schools and in your public places, people are trained to show every human being dignity and get up every day and say, "Everybody I see, I'm going to see God in. I'm going to see God in everybody I see today." Let that be the way you wake up every day. I'm going to see God in every single person I see today.

The thing that's really—that makes me cry when I think about it… These young men…the young women, too, but it really touches me with these tough guys, you know. I'm sure a policeman would see Tory and Damian and some of these guys on the street and say, "That's Mike Brown." You know? I can't tell you what it means to me when they see me and they give me a big hug: "Hey, Rabbi." It is the most humbling thing in the world to me. It means everything to me. Everything, and I don't want to betray that trust. I want to earn that every day. I want to earn that every day, and everybody can do that. You see a young black man in the street, you look him in the eye and smile at him and say, "Have a good day," because they don't get that a lot.

Go out into the World

Renita Lamkin, the pastor of St. John's AME Church in St. Charles, Missouri, shares some of her reflections of her congregation's awakening to their relationship to young people in their community.

I remember feeling ill—I felt like I had been punched in the gut or some kind of weight was inside me. So I started texting some friends. We were kind of back and forth chatting about what was going on—and I just needed more information about what was happening. I was not familiar with Ferguson at all. I never had a reason to drive through Ferguson. I've really never been in the community, just had no reason to be there. Still, I felt this overwhelming sense of grief. My kids were out of town and suddenly I felt this incredible need to be with them and hear their voices.

This all reminded me of when Trayvon Martin was murdered and how helpless I felt then. I was out of town and the kids were at home and I felt the same urgency to be with them.

At that time, I was in school full-time. I was parenting. I was working. I was all of this, and I didn't have the time to do anything. I don't even know what there would have been to do, but I didn't have the ability to do anything but write, so I wrote about white privilege and the way black kids are treated and shared some of my son's experiences.

I felt that sinking feeling—the one that is felt every time you hear sirens and wonder "Is that my kid?" Even though that thought just crosses your mind real fast, the fact is that it's always there. It was like suddenly all of the anger that I have not been able to express because life has been too busy came to the forefront. All of the times my son was brought home by the police because he was riding his bike in the neighborhood, or was the black kid that was put on the city bus because he's black and of course he lives in the city. I just didn't have the wherewithal to fight the system back then. I didn't have the fight in me because there's so much fighting for everyday life that I couldn't engage the bigger fight.

But now I'm at this place. The kids are gone from home. Life is less chaotic. I'm finished with school, and I had the space to be mad and to be sad and to be aware and to act. I didn't know what to do. I just knew that I needed to be where the young folks were. I needed to be with them.

On Wednesday [Aug.13], the AMEs were going to go do this march. So I'm like "ah-ha. I'll go with the group, and I'll figure it out," and that's what I did. So this is where I kind of got launched into whatever this was that I was doing. The march and rally ended, and it was time for everybody to get out of the street. And people were like, "Why do we have to get out of the street? We're not gonna get out of the street." The police kept saying, "You guys got to get your people out of the street," and so the preachers were running around trying to get people out of the street and pretty much everybody had cleared the street. But there was this one young girl who was so distraught, and she planted herself in the middle of the street, and she was genuinely distraught, and she wasn't going to move.

There was lots of attention on her and around her. She didn't want to be photographed so I stood there blocking the cameras and yelling at photographers. People were yelling at her to get out of the street—I think I yelled at them to leave her alone. My sense was that she was grieving and just needed some space.

I was so engaged with this that I don't remember hearing the tanks come down the street, was so engaged with whatever this was. But when the tanks came, that's when everybody surged into the streets. Now, there were people who were already in the streets and weren't going to get out, but the tanks came and just about everybody came into the streets., The police were in the line, and there were some young folks that were pretty determined that they were going to charge through that police line—to go where, to do what, I am uncertain. One of the unfortunate things about that was that there were people who were coming home on the bus, and they were just trying to get home, and the police wouldn't let them by. People wanted to get back to their cars, and the police wouldn't let them by. So these things caused more tension and more anger in the crowd. In addition, we could hear the dogs barking in the tank.

So now you hear these dogs barking in the tanks. You've these police in this military gear on top of the tank with the machine gun. Is it a real gun? I don't know. Is it a periscope? Are they just looking? I don't know. But it sure looks like he's standing up there with a machine gun. Those are the images. Somehow I had this determination, everybody goes home tonight. That was the goal. Police and people, everybody goes home. They're not going to be injured, and the people aren't going to be injured. Everybody's going home. So I drew a line in the spirit and called on the angels to stand with me – to stand with the people and keep evil from unleashing.

Sometimes somebody would say, "Who are you with? Whose side are you on?" I'd say, "I'm on life's side." Whose side are you on? Life. Are you with the police? I'm with Jesus.

I'm compelled by the fact that the church has so many opportunities to be the presence of love and life and too often we reject those opportunities. Our church actually went through a paradigm shift and a transformation some years ago when one of our young guys was killed. He died of an alcohol-induced seizure. While I'm dealing with these funeral arrangements, there was so much talk about whether he wears a suit or doesn't wear a suit. I heard stories about how active he had been in church at one time – yet there was this very broken relationship with the church. He was like this generation that we've shamed. They didn't want to wear "church" clothes, and they wear hats, and they say this, that, and the other—and so we exclude them.

One day, when I was doing a home visit at this young man's mom's house, he wanted to walk me to my car when I was leaving, and he showed me this tattoo on his chest. This is what he wanted to do. He wanted to show me this tattoo where he had Jesus on his chest. He says, "I don't know how to keep him in me, so I got him on me. So I can remember." And now this kid is laying in a coffin—and the fight is about whether or not he wears a suit. At…the end of the day, does anybody care? If we could have gone back 20 years and said, "You know what? If a suit is going to be what separates you from God, then come in your shorts."

This experience took our church through a transition from being this very stale and quiet proper church to anything but that. Now, people who want to wear fancy church clothes wear fancy church clothes, and people who don't, don't, and we're all okay with that. Everyone is embraced and loved—genuinely. It took time and work—but we got there.

To really be with people rejected by the church, we have to be willing to be vulnerable, and we have to be willing to be inappropriate to our colleagues and our peers. We even have to risk being rejected by the ones we are attempting to love. We have to be willing to care less about what other people think about us and only be concerned about what people are thinking about God through us. We have to ask ourselves, "What are we causing people to think about God?" Romans 8:35, says, "Who shall separate us from the love of God?" We have to look at what we were doing to separate people from the love of God. Shall hats in the pews separate us from the love of God? Shall sagging pants separate us from the love of God? Shall bandanas on our face separate us from the love of God? Shall traditions, church leaders, or doctrines?

The way that people know the love of God is by how we engage them, and so we have to look at what are we doing to separate people from experiencing God. We have to be willing to accept that we share responsibility in the relationship that people desire to have with God – this is s one thing that has become very clear.

I believe that if the church is going to really be effective in this world, we have to be willing to be where the people are and understand that the church is not just the place to bring the sinners to get saved. The church is the place to bring the saved to be empowered, to go out into the world and be love.

Rebecca Ragland talking with a police officer on behalf of an arrested protestor outside of a St. Louis Rams football game. *(AP photo)*

Starsky Wilson prays during the prayer vigil for wounded officers on March 12, 2015. *(Photo by Laurie Skrivan*/St. Louis Post-Dispatch/*Polaris)*

CHAPTER 10

#staywoke

"Arise, shine; for your light has come..."

Isaiah 60:1a (NRSV)

In 1966, Martin Luther King, Jr., delivered a speech during a Universalist Unitarian General Assembly meeting titled "Don't Sleep Through the Revolution." Dr. King's speech was a clarion call for the church to remain awake to the social injustices of the day, and join the Civil Rights Movement's efforts to eradicate unjust racial and economic systems in the United States and around the globe. King gave this speech one year after "Bloody Sunday" occurred in Selma, Alabama, where peaceful protestors campaigning for voting rights for African Americans were met with violent opposition from police and civilians. The images from "Bloody Sunday," coupled with Dr. King's invitation, compelled hundreds of clergy from around the country to go to Selma and join the struggle for voting rights.

A contingent of clergy from St. Louis responded to the call. Cardinal Joseph Ritter, Archbishop of St. Louis, secured a chartered plane through the Archdiocese of St. Louis and led an interfaith group of 48 people to Selma. Sister Antona Ebo, a Franciscan Sister of Mary, was invited to join the group. She was the only African American woman on this trip, and in her recent visit to Ferguson, she compared some of the rhetoric related to the young activists in Ferguson to the accusations about Selma protestors in 1965, and draws on her faith tradition to frame what it means to do right in this instance. In a recent interview she said, "When the young blacks in Ferguson speak, they are rabble-rousers, and that's what we were called when we went to Selma. We were called rabble-rousers and dupes of the communists because (FBI director) J. Edgar Hoover was working so hard to prove that Martin Luther King was not a Christian but a communist. People who had put their trust in J. Edgar Hoover rather than J.C..—if only they would have put their trust in J.C., they would have been on the right side of this thing. It's the same kind of stuff that's happening now."[1]

What is happening now is people are waking up to the realities of the racial disparities in the United States and their impact on black communities. For instance, the Mother 2 Mother events gained so much traction in St. Louis because so many white mothers were saying they had no idea so many black mothers' sons encountered such discrimination in schools, neighborhoods, and with the police. At each gathering, a white mother would inevitably ask, "So what can we do about this?" and earnestly desire concrete answers. There is not simply one answer, because this is a complex problem that requires a multifaceted solution. The conversation would often turn toward asking, "What circumstances are within your immediate control?" In other words, what kinds of actions can you take today to bring about racial justice in our country? Each time, white mothers were challenged to reflect on their own interactions with African Americans, and how often their children had meaningful interaction with them, such as going over to their homes and vice-versa. White mothers were also asked to think about the message sent to their children if they do not have any meaningful interactions with African Americans.

The goal is not to just be able to say, "I have black friends," but to genuinely seek to be in relationship with people who are racially different in an attempt to move beyond stereotypes and build authentic community. In her book *The Journey Is Home,* Nelle Morton talks about the process of "hearing to speech" when we acknowledge people by giving them our full attention, and being willing to hear them speak their truth, in their way, and on their terms.[2] Hearing people to speech doesn't only value the process of speaking, but the content of the message. We must first see people as valued human beings who are deserving of being heard, then making space for their voices to be heard, and be willing to contend with the truths that emerge.

[1]http://stlouisreview.com/article/2014-10-15/sister-antona-ebo accessed December 2, 2014.
[2]Nelle Morton, *The Journey Is Home* (Boston: Beacon Press, 1985), 202.

As the young activists have shown, they created space to hear each other to speech, even when others did not want to hear them. Their resolve and determination called forth the best out of the clergy and faith communities that supported them. During the prayer vigil after the two police officers were shot near the Ferguson police station, Osagyefo Sekou, a clergy activist who is a St. Louis native, offered one of the prayers that evening. His task was to pray for the young activists, and brought their plight into the center of the gathering.

Loving God, we say, "Thank you for these young people who have come to the streets and who have reminded us of the rich tradition of which made this very gathering possible, for those young people who have been mocked and betrayed by every level of government, who have often been betrayed by the homes of which they have come from, but these young who demanded that the world place on its lips three simple words that are pregnant with the possibilities of American democracy, these young people who remind us that 'black life matters.'"

And so, God, for them, we say, "Thank you." For 200 some odd days, they have been demonized, and they have been mocked, and they have been called names. But, nevertheless, they stand up, and, when they stand up, the best of who we are stands up with them. And so, God, now, we pray that a hedge of protection might be around them and that their hearts might be filled with a deep, abiding love that hate will never have the last word, but that they might know that they are not—that they are loved and that they are cared for and that there are people around them who believe in them, O God.

For we have seen you in their faces, O God. We have seen you when they scream and they yell and they are angry. We have seen the very face of God in them. We have seen that God has tattoos on God's face and that God sags God's pants and that God loves us so much that God is willing to stand in front of tanks and tear gas and bear witness to a truth that they will not bow down. And so, for them, we pray, and we say, "Thank you, thank you, thank you for these young people who have made us all a little more courageous, who have made us all a little more angry, and who have made us all a little more considerate that we must do our work with a deep, abiding love."

And, God, for those who languish in jails, we pray for them For those who have been hurt in anger, we pray for them—and, God, that they might know. So right now, we call you to account for your word. We say over them that they may be persecuted, but they are not forsaken—that they are fearfully and wonderfully made in the very workmanship of God.

That they might know that they are loved, O God; for, Lord, we know their prayer and their actions might be the salvation of this nation. All of this, we ask in your name. Amen.

The racial disparities that the Ferguson events have laid bare are part of a complex system of injustice that requires a multifaceted approach to correct it. The stories in this book point to some of the "signposts," as Diana Butler Bass calls them, that, if nurtured, can lead us along a pathway toward racial justice.[3] Although Bass is primarily talking about practices that congregations do to form them to join God's work in the world, the clergy who have engaged in the movement for racial justice have actually *joined* God's work in the world and created a new set of signposts that point us in the direction of racial justice.

Clergy practices of prayer created an awakening to the presence of God in unlikely places. The "altars" were moved out of the sanctuaries and onto the streets, where they challenged people to see, hear, and feel the presence of God in the midst of the protests. The chanting, marching, and locking arms often symbolized a resolute strength and power that challenged us to consider why black lives mattered to God, and why they should matter to us all. The struggle for human dignity is a deeply theological issue, for to be human is to be created in the image of God, and whenever one's humanity is distorted or discounted, it is an affront to God. Clergy were right to call the struggle to be treated as fully human as the work of God, and they affirmed this truth each time they showed up at protests in their robes, stoles, and collars.

Clergy practices of risk-taking were present each time they risked their personal safety, emotional well-being, or financial stability. To lay one's collar on the altar of justice is to take a tremendous risk, because it is not the popular or easy road to travel. Clergy bodies in the streets stood in solidarity with the aims of the movement, but they

---

[3]Diana Butler Bass, *Christianity for the Rest of Us: How the Neighborhood Church Is Transforming the Faith* (New York: Harper One, 2006), 11.

often served as buffers between the police and other protestors. Some were tear-gassed and others shot with rubber bullets, yet those safety risks were secondary to their commitment to the fight for racial justice. The emotional risk of losing friends and acquaintances because they (the ministers) were no longer seen as "respectable" standing alongside the protestors did not cause them to waiver. And the financial risk of angering congregants who expressed their anger by threatening to withhold donations and recommend they be fired were part of some of the clergy's lived experiences.

Clergy practices of creating safe sanctuary took on new meaning and opportunity. Many denominations have "safe sanctuary"-type policies that congregations are expected to adhere to in order to ensure the safety and well-being of children and youth. While those policies are needed and important, the clergy in this movement expanded our collective imagination about the ways in which our sanctuaries can become safe havens for the movement for racial justice. They opened their doors for meetings and consultations. They offered their kitchens for meal prep and service. They provided cots and cups of water for wayfaring travelers. Their sanctuaries were safe for all people—regardless of age, race, ability, or sexual orientation. Few had to worry about being made to feel unwelcome because they didn't fit a prescribed image of a "respectable" person. These sanctuaries were havens of physical and emotional safety.

The clergy's practice of "letting go" enabled them to step aside so there could be room for young leaders to step up front. Many clergy are accustomed to taking charge and leading the way for others to follow. In this movement, leadership took on a different form that made room for "the first to be last" and "the last to be first." Often the clergy would follow the lead of the young people by listening to them, offering advice when warranted, and giving them space to find their own voices. They supported, affirmed, and prayed for the young activists. They apologized for the way many faith communities have not been havens or refuges for them in the past. They let go of being in charge and acquiesced to what they understood God to be doing in their midst through others.

These practices of prayer, risk-taking, creating safe sanctuary, and letting go were emblematic of the clergy engagement in this movement for racial justice. These "street signposts" are the kinds of activities that could be regularly witnessed for any who cared to see. They point us toward the embodiment of being God's love in the world, and challenge us to consider making them part of our own faith practice.

The "street signposts" also challenge us to consider the opportunities for faith communities in the wake of Ferguson—to join the quest for racial justice around the country. As previously mentioned, Ferguson is merely one example of the racial injustice that is present in cities and towns around the United States, not an anomaly. This is a moral injustice, and faith communities are still being called upon to frame it as such. Now that we have been awakened to these injustices, there are at least three things we must do to #staywoke in order to be able to demand systemic changes that promote the fair and equitable treatment of black people. We must awaken to the awareness of our own privilege, build relationships in our own communities, and connect this awareness and the corresponding action in order to effect change for a more racially just world.

Awakening to white privilege, or benefits bestowed upon white people that non-white people do not receive, is crucial to the cause for racial justice. Cultural critic and educator Tim Wise makes the case for why people must be awakened to white privilege. He writes, "Being a member of the majority, the dominant group, allows one to ignore how race shapes one's life. For those of us called white, whiteness simply is. Whiteness becomes, for us, the unspoken, interrogated norm, taken for granted, much as water can be taken for granted by a fish."[4] The realities of white privilege can be as difficult to see as the air we breathe. Our cultural and social norms are shaped by it, yet mostly those who do not readily benefit from it see its prevalence in our society.

It is unlikely for a white person to be racially profiled. Even though "whiteness" is a race, it is rarely characterized as such, while "blackness" is readily deemed a race and too often evokes suspicion and distrust. African Americans have long been subject to unwarranted traffic stops. "Driving while black" is a reason that many have come to give for the disproportionate number of black people who are stopped by police. According to the Missouri Attorney General's 2013 report, black drivers were 66 percent more likely to be stopped by the police than other drivers.[5] This is merely one example out of many of the ways black people are assumed to be suspicious simply because they are black.

It is no wonder the #usemeinstead social media campaign emerged in January 2015 after the discovery of a Florida police department's

---

[4]Tim Wise, *White Like Me: Reflections on Race from a Privileged Son* (Berkeley, Calif.: Soft Skull Press, 2011), 2.

[5]http://www.stltoday.com/news/local/crime-and-courts/new-stats-but-same-trend-on-missouri-traffic-stops/article_77bec173-fbf3-563e-bd73-16538701d5bd.html accessed January 15, 2015.

use of black men's mugshots for target practice.[6] A group of Lutheran clergy decided to submit photos of themselves to the police department for target practice use, and the movement spread to include clergy of many denominations. These mostly white clergy challenged the police department to use their pictures, in clergy garb, for target practice instead of black men. If shooting the pictures of black men was an acceptable practice, they believed using their pictures should be acceptable as well. And if not, why not?

"Whiteness" also allows most white people to not immediately be deemed out of place, or not belonging in the everyday places they visit. A few years ago our family lived in Webster Groves, Missouri, which is a relatively affluent suburb of St. Louis. It is chock full of beautiful homes, tree-lined streets, and quaint shops and restaurants. One sunny day, my husband and I decided to put our kids in their wagon and walk to the local ice cream parlor. On the way back home, we walked past a restaurant whose outdoor seating was full of patrons. All of the sudden we heard, "Well, that's a *strange* sight!" *Strange?* There are three primary modes of transportation in this town: cars, bikes, and wagons. What is *strange* about a father pulling his kids in a wagon in Webster Groves? I see it all the time. Surely this was about more than a father pulling his kids in a wagon. Although my example cannot be compared to the instances of racial profiling that have led to the emotional and physical torture of the victim, it does point to the more subtle ways that racial bias can emerge in an ordinary situation.

Recognizing white privilege is a step toward using it as a resource to bring about a more just and equitable world. Julie Taylor, a Unitarian Universalist community minister and active participant in the protest movement, reflects on her own understanding of white privilege, and how faith communities should be places of its deconstruction.

What are you doing to dismantle that systemic racism where you are? Where that means, as white people, we have to give up the comfort and the privilege that we have. And so, where's the work around knowing that we have privilege and being willing to give it up? No matter what our race, we are all embedded in white supremacy and white privilege in this country because

[6]http://www.washingtonpost.com/news/morning-mix/wp/2015/01/25/florida-police-used-mugshots-of-black-men-for-target-practice-clergy-responded-usemeinstead/ accessed January 29, 2015.

it is the air that we breathe. And so, noticing that is the first piece, and acknowledging that is the truth is the first step—and understanding it may not be personally about you. For example, when white people say "Well, I had it hard growing up, so I don't have white privilege. I had to work for everything I had." That conversation, I'm tired of having, but it's the one that has to keep happening, I think, for white people to get it.

I did not have it easy coming up. We were a missionary family. Of the money my parents raised for the mission board, they were allowed to keep $485 a month. That's what we lived on from 1970 until 1980. We didn't grow up with much of anything, but I still have white privilege.

I think congregations may need to be a place—if we can get enough leaders, whether it's clergy leaders or lay leaders—that can start figuring out for themselves how to unpack those pieces of how white privilege works in our society. Congregations and faith communities are meant for and typically work as such great places of healing. Maybe we need to start changing the language. Instead of "dismantling the systems" of racism and white privilege, maybe we've got to talk about "healing the systems." Maybe that's what it is for people of faith who keep struggling with this idea... See how we can heal it, because it is not healthy, the way we live. The healing must happen on a deeper level. The systems are a by-product of the illness of racism and classism, not the cause of it. Sometimes healing requires taking apart, uprooting, dislodging, dismantling the unhealthy elements. So the more I think about it, the more I want to be clear that I think racism and classism are the pieces that must be healed, and those are individual and internal, before any healing of a structure can take place. If we dismantle the systems without doing the work of healing, we will create new dysfunctional and oppressive structures.

I wish I had an answer about how to make this happen. For me, I have to start my healing with awareness and willingness to live in discomfort due to my complicity in white supremacy and privilege. Now that I'm "woke" to this, I can't keep it to myself. I am compelled to point to it, preach about it, talk to people about it, talk to white people. Essentially, be a race traitor. And since I am a parent, I need to embody and model this so my children will internalize it. I would love to think I can change the world, but it may be that I really only have the ability to change my house. Otherwise I need to be a follower in this Movement.

In St. Louis, organizations such as Metropolitan Congregations United (MCU), an interdenominational organization of religious congregations, work with local faith communities to help improve the quality of life on a local, regional, and state level. David Gerth, the Executive Director of MCU, describes the focus of their work and how it has evolved over the past few years.

We're ecumenical and interfaith based in the city and the county. We've been around for almost 25 years now, and the reason that we were founded was because congregations in neighborhoods that were changing recognized that they wanted to have an impact on what was happening in their neighborhoods. And this was still at a point where congregations were more and more commuter, but there was still a sense of connection to the neighborhood. And, over these 20 plus years, we've grown as we've recognized that fighting social justice issues at the neighborhood level leads you to look at what's going on in the ward or in the city and, ultimately, in the region, the state, and the nation.

And so we have gone through evolutions where we have spent a lot more time on regional and state issues than on neighborhood issues, and there's always been a tension for us about that. And it's been an acute tension for the last couple of years because, when you work on broad issues, sometimes people have a hard time figuring out, well, "What's in it for me?" This issue is very, very powerful from an organizing perspective because many of us see this as down the street, on my corner level of an issue that has regional and state and federal implications.

So the issues that we work on emerge from what is most important to our member congregations and, to some extent, to the partner organizations that we ally ourselves with. Sometimes, we're influenced by those ally relationships, too, but it's basically what's important to our folks. And what's historically been important to our folks is equity—economic equity has always been right at the center, along with racial equity and how that plays out in what people call the social determinants of health.

Our national network, Gamaliel, had always had this clear focus on economic and racial equity. Also, it had a couple of internal crisis points over the years. Maybe about 10 years ago we had a major kind of moment of reflection about how our own internal racism was impacting our work. And so there was some very sophisticated strategic planning done that changed the way we organized the body, the way we govern and so forth. And, about two years ago, people started saying that, in this phase of this current strategic plan, it was time to come back and actually really focus on race and racism.

A second point for faith communities considering joining the movement for racial justice is to build relationships in their own communities, especially with young people. David Gerth reflects on the way some of the clergy relationships formed with the young activists.

The first night on the street, Alexis and Brittany, after they stopped chanting, they were sitting in the street, and then they were just like any ordinary twenty-somethings. They were thanking everybody and hugging people and saying, "We were just standing behind you." We're like, "You're the ones that were doing the work." But it meant something to them that we were there and we could start to see—and that just escalated. The more we did together and the more that we were backing them up, the more that there was an opportunity for us not to be the ones with all the answers but to be in actual relationship, at least to get closer to where we're actually having a relationship rather than figuring either that the old people are clueless or the young people are clueless, which is kind of how I think we all approached it at the beginning.

Being a caring and considerate presence can help build trust and form community. Derrick Robinson, pastor of Kingdom Dominion Church, immediately connected with young people in the early days of the movement, and discusses how he cultivated those relationships to help build community.

When we were at the Ferguson police station the day after Mike was killed, I went over to share with the young people, to kind of encourage and just let them know we're here to support, that we're all in this together. I had on my collar that day and the trust was not there. It was like, we don't want to listen to you. We don't want you to be around us. We don't want you to even speak to us. All you all want to come and force your Jesus on us. We've had that Jesus.

So I said, "Let me show you. Let me show you how Jesus can be. Let me show you how Jesus was among the people. Let me show you how Jesus walked from judgment hall to judgment hall. Let me show you how Jesus exemplified being a leader in front of the people."

That's what really thrust me into getting involved, and that was really my view as it relates to being a pastor in the community. I think you've got to be able to be among the people. After that, I felt compelled. I felt young people wanting to fight. I felt young people wanting to have a voice. I felt young people wanting to make a stand. I felt my role would be more of an assistant to them, more of a mentor to them, and, even some, I'm more of a father to them. There are many sons that I've come out of this movement with, many who call me "Dad." It was one of the things that I knew the assignment that God told me to go to…was to the boys on the street, boys who don't listen to our typical church "riddles." I felt that I needed to tap into them, and that's what I felt my assignment was—to be more of a mentor to them.

One of my closest mentees hated me in the beginning. He was like, "I don't talk to no preachers." He said, "I don't deal with preachers." And I went back to him the next couple of hours, and I talked to him. I started sharing things with him, just about the community and just about life in general, just building conversation.

And as I built conversation I think that's how I was able to eventually make the change—but also by becoming "proven" by the young people. When they…tested you, and they found you consistent or they found that your word became who you are, they found that something you've done for them, not financially but just being there for them. They found you consistent, and that's what builds trust in the community, and that's how I was able to build trust in the community.

We started to take some out to eat. We would take some to a place called Blank Space in St. Louis where they would do poetry, listen to music. Just kind of sit there, let them mellow out. I wanted to make them feel comfortable. So we'd just take them to the mall, kind of walk around with them.

And I think that's what the church's focus has to be. How can we make a community impact? How can we change the lives of the young people that stay three miles from our church, or around the corner? Everybody in that two miles should know who the pastors are. I think it's very crucial because when people know that it's just not a building there, but things are actually happening within the community, the church will begin to emerge in the community as a leader. And I think, also, the church has to make sure that we get back to our number one focus. That's changing lives. If we don't change lives, then we don't need to exist.

Dietra Baker, pastor of Liberation Christian Church (DOC) presses the importance of fostering relationships within one's own communities.

I think a lot of us, at heart, we want to do something. We're always talking about something, but something about this movement forced us to be the hands and feet for the Christians and Jesus, forces to be incarnate in ways that we were struggling to get to. And I think that the incarnation will help us move back into areas really of long-term work where we're gifted differently and need to continue to move the work forward together.

[This movement] also changed our relationships with each other in generally a good way. The clergy in the city have never been as close as they are now. I'm glad that I had a little bit of a part of that. We have some relationships that we didn't have before, which we should have. I mean, it's pretty central to our faith, but we didn't have them, and we could tell when we tried to start doing stuff together that we didn't know each other and that we didn't have relationships with each other. We didn't know each other as deeply as we needed to to be able to do what God was calling us to do.

The most heartbreaking thing early on and even in these crisis points during the indictment decision time—it was really obviously the churches that were in Ferguson, a lot of them weren't connected to the community. I didn't hop up and say to Liberation, "Let's go build community with people in Ferguson." I said to Liberation, "We need to be on deck here in our neighborhood." It's a signpost to the rest of us. How deep are your relationships with people in the neighborhood?

If something goes off in the neighborhood, is somebody going to come to Liberation and say, "I know that church. I know that pastor. I know those people. They care."? And we're the church that says we're going to liberate lives and liberate communities, so we need to walk the walk. So that was a wakeup call, that we didn't really have the deep kind of relationships with the community—besides trying to save people or evangelize people. We didn't have the respect or the trust or the honor because, when you do right in the community, there's an honor there. There's a respect there. There's a knowing there. There's a trust there. We'll come to you, and we'll partner with you, and we'll be with you in certain situations.

And so there was a period where we really had to say [to the young people], "Hey, we messed up. We haven't built the kind of relationships that we should have been building with you, and let's build them and keep moving forward." And then, my call to liberators and to other clergy is, "Make sure you don't miss this lesson. Go build in your community. Make sure the neighbors in your community know you."

A final reflection on the ways in which faith communities can join the quest for racial justice is to remain awake, and connect these learnings to the systemic issues and utilize them to effect change. Christopher

Potter, an Episcopal Service Corp intern from Massachusetts, reflects on the kind of tension he experienced that could only be resolved by getting engaged in the movement for racial justice.

> The kingdom of God is not a white kingdom,...nor is it a colorblind kingdom. I believe that God's vision for us, as individuals, is for us to reach our fullest potential and be able to grow into our full selves and not be misshapen by evil or oppression. And so, for us, as ministers—clergy and laypeople, we're all ministers—we have to actively break down systems that prevent people from reaching their full humanity in all aspects for...if a black person is being oppressed, they're not able to fully express all aspects of their identity. People should be able to grow into whatever identity they have. That's when we'll really start seeing the kingdom exist on earth.
>
> The thing that struck me about the first action, the prayer on the sidewalk, was the raw emotion of the black teens who were there. It had already been like a month or two, and they were, like, chanting until they were hoarse like it had happened yesterday. And that created a lot of tension for me because when people are striving for dignity and safety, you can't really stay neutral. If you don't do anything to help, you're essentially against them. So a lot of tension like that could only be resolved by supporting them in some way in having their rights...met: to do nothing was not an option.

Martin Geiger, another Episcopal Service Corp intern from Illinois, connects his learnings to his broader sense of calling and vocation that is rooted in the church and gives expression through tangible acts of love, justice, and mercy.

> So I think one of the things that's really central to the work of the church is reconciliation and, specifically, like, the drawing and healing of communities that have been fractured by power and the ways it's misused. One of the things that became really clear to me through being in Ferguson and living here and hearing these stories is that police violence is really real, and it's a key

weapon that gets used on behalf of power to keep itself in power, to close communities off.

So I grew up and went to school in university towns where that was not necessarily as obvious, but I think it was very much present. I was just kind of shielded from it because I was one of the people being protected by that [police] violence. So stepping into the street and realizing, like, "Oh, this is like we've given this particular group of people this incredible power of violence and we justified it through the state," just felt so immediately wrong, like such a huge barrier to real reconciliation in the community happening. I don't see how the church can do its work without making an effort to change a system of violence. I mean, I think that's what Christ's atonement is all about, certainly,...that resistance to systems of violence.

One of the things that I've been working out while I've been here is what feels, at the moment, at least, like a call to the priesthood. So I've been starting to think through that process. And one of the things that being present in Ferguson and seeing how a lot of local clergy were involved in the work there made clear to me was that work in the church as a priest could be an act of resistance, that it wasn't—that I didn't have—that it wasn't just like signing onto this nice like country club and helping people, which I think it's really easy to fall into a vision of the church where the church exists primarily to uphold the status quo.

And the church has fallen into that a lot, especially perhaps the Episcopal Church. But I think watching priests and clergy from all sorts of traditions get involved and get into the streets and really, explicitly use their privilege, as members of the clergy, to protect others, like, I think has been really powerful and really inspiring and helped me really reshape what I think, like, ordination is capable of doing for people, so I'm in. The fact that it was so explicit that protestors would say, "Okay, we want clergy here because that restrains the police," like, I was realizing, "Oh, wait, like, there's really good things you can do with the privilege of wearing the collar."

Rebecca Ragland, pastor of The Episcopal Church of the Holy Communion, makes explicit the role of the church in staying awake, and the ways our connections extend beyond the local faith community and into the wider world to connect with others on the same road toward justice.

We, as the church, we all are committed to the common cause of justice and so we are seeing where each person's "giftings" are and their capacities and so we're naming those and making sure they're brought forth and aware of each other's incapacities and weaknesses and the deep need that we all have for each other.

For example, "Momma Cat" had a dinner for us at Christmastime. All the protestors were there. Momma Cat is a woman who is unbelievable. She has been at the protests faithfully since the day after Mike Brown died. She is a 4.0 culinary school person. She's just graduating this month and so she can cook like nobody's business and make cakes that are just gorgeous. She would go home and cook meals for the protestors and come out and feed them, faithfully feed them. And not just feed them macaroni and cheese out of a box. I mean seriously feed them. She is a beautiful person. And she has been so faithful and so committed and she identifies the needs of who can do what. There's just really this sense of "who does what" in this community.

I know maybe 40 or 50 people who I really genuinely care about and want to see on a regular basis. I didn't know any of them in August, and now, I know all these people and I'm in community with them. And there was this sense of, like, "Wow, that's church growth." So how to kind of capture that sense of common working together, identifying each other's giftedness and the power of persecution to grow community is something I had never seen before.

What I've learned from this experience and I'm continuing to learn is that clergy have to heed the call to stay awake. It's so easy in this vocation to be so busy that you get into the drone of beating your wings and getting the honey, or however you want to think about the metaphor of work of being a pastor, that you can forget to stay awake to the wider issues that you're truly called to. And staying awake is also critically important for us in our communities because we need to open our eyes and see the systems and keep aware, so that we can raise up leadership.

I am just more and more deeply aware of how I've been asleep— asleep to how the decisions and apathy in this moment are going to critically affect next year and the decade ahead because we're not raising up leaders in our church who are going to run for election and so we're just going to get fed who our leaders are going to be. We don't have to do that, and we aren't awake to the legislation. We're not awake to all of these ways in which decisions are made. And I realize there's a separation of church and state, but we are embodiments of the culture around us. And if we are asleep, we aren't able to participate and embody the change that we want to see. I think that's a critical thing both for pastors and for people in the church.

Karen Anderson, pastor of Ward Chapel AME Church, reflects on the ways in which she implored her congregation to remain awake and connect with what is happening in the community.

I think this was also a time when sermons changed a bit. I think that I've always preached with a view towards liberation and history, but I think they changed a bit because I felt a greater need to talk about the oneness of the community and the fact that this was an issue that affected all of us, whether we were directly involved or not, and trying to show the connection to the community that we have because I think, sometimes, when we don't live in a situation and it does not affect us, we become desensitized to the violence around us. I think I felt a push to make us aware of the violence around us; and to talk about it and to preach about it, but to preach about it from the standpoint of restoration, to speak about it from the standpoint of liberation, to speak about it from the standpoint of "Ubuntu," the African proverb that says "I am because we are." We're in this thing together and...we have to have a voice;...the church can't be silent anymore.

I think...another connection was I also talked again about the history of our church and that the history of the church was born from protests—that it was a protest against the inability to worship freely, and that, if it had not been for the courage of people to protest, the AME Church would not exist and so we're called to speak against things that hold us in oppression. And I felt a need to do that, too, because the congregation began to realize that I was involved, and they were concerned for my safety. And so I had to speak to them about why I was there.

I told them I was there because I felt called to be there and that I felt that that's a part of the gospel I believe, that I have to be present, that it's not enough for me to sit in the church and talk about what needs to happen, that I have to take an active role in what is happening.

"Taking an active role in what is happening" was a primary theme from all of the clergy who engaged in this movement. The vision of a future filled with hope is clearly demonstrated by the clergy, but young activists first brought it to light. They are the people who held the line, claimed the streets as their own, and demanded to be treated as full human beings. These young activists are the ones whose righteous indignation often inspired the clergy to support these efforts, and awakened the spirit of possibility that challenged our prescribed notions of community and drew the circle wide to model a community that is emblematic of God's love and grace.

As faith communities, the ball is in our court. Will we wake up and #staywoke, or will we fall prey to sleeping through this revolution? Do we join this modeling of community whose base is wide enough to genuinely welcome all people regardless of race, social class, gender, age, differing abilities, sexuality, and religion? ? Or do we hold onto prescribed notions that box us into a corner and only allow us to play ball with people with whom we feel most comfortable? Are we willing to risk being uncomfortable in order to excavate the roots of prejudice in our hearts and minds so that we can truly build beloved community? Do we take seriously the need to clean off and refocus the lenses through which we see black people so all people can be seen as full human beings who are created in the image of God?

The fight for racial justice emerges out of the fight for human dignity. If there is any group of people who should be compelled to join this fight, it is the people who call themselves "children of God." Staying awake to the injustices that have been revealed through the Ferguson-related events is a critical task for communities of faith. Our connectedness to our brothers and sisters is rooted in our connectedness to God, for we are all God's children. And, in the words of the Civil Rights freedom fighter Ella Baker:

> Until the killing of black men, black mothers' sons, becomes as important to the rest of the country as the killing of a white mother's son—we who believe in freedom cannot rest until this happens.

Mothers' March candlelight vigil in Clayton on November 1, 2014. *(Photo by Cristina Fletes-Boutte/*St. Louis Post-Dispatch/*Polaris)*

Sister Antona Ebo, who marched in Selma, Alabama, in 1965, visits Ferguson in August, 2014, and is greeted by Missouri State Highway Patrol Captain Ron Johnson. *(Photo by Philip Deitch)*

Protestors march on West Florissant Avenue in Ferguson. *(Photo by Julie Taylor)*

Ferguson Commission member Rasheen Aldridge.
(Photo by Wiley Price/St. Louis American)

Index

About the Author

Dr. Leah Gunning Francis is the Associate Dean for Contextual Education and Assistant Professor of Christian Education at Eden Theological Seminary in St. Louis, Missouri.

A frequent guest lecturer, preacher, and workshop facilitator, she draws on her marketing experience, pastoral leadership and academic training to creatively equip students, clergy, and congregations for transformative social action.

Dr. Gunning Francis earned a Bachelor of Science degree in Marketing from Hampton University; a Master of Divinity degree from Candler School of Theology at Emory University; and a Doctor of Philosophy degree from Garrett-Evangelical Theological Seminary.

A native of Willingboro, New Jersey, Dr. Gunning Francis is married to Rev. Rodney Francis, Senior Pastor of Washington Tabernacle Baptist Church. They live with their children in St. Louis.